PENGUIN  CLASSICS

STUNG WITH LOVE

SAPPHO was born after 630 BCE and died around 570. A native of the island of Lesbos, she resided in its largest city, Mytilene. Though a poet of considerable range, she is best known for amatory poems focusing on adolescent females. After her death she became a figure of legend and, in the Hellenistic period (323–146 BCE), was canonized as one of the nine lyric poets worthy of study. Though little of her poetry survived the Middle Ages, archaeological excavation has recovered numerous fragments. She is renowned as the first woman poet in literary history.

AARON POOCHIGIAN attended Moorhead State University in Moorhead, Minnesota, 1991–6, where he studied under the poets Dave Mason, Alan Sullivan and Tim Murphy. He entered graduate school for Classics in 1997 at the University of Minnesota, Twin Cities. After travelling and doing research in Greece on fellowship, 2003–4, he earned his PhD in 2006. His original poems have appeared in such journals as *Arion*, *Dark Horse* and *Poetry Magazine*.

CAROL ANN DUFFY is a British poet, playwright and freelance writer. Her poetry has received every major award in Britain, including the Whitbread and Forward Prizes for *Mean Time* and the T. S. Eliot Award for *Rapture*. In the USA she has received the E. M. Forster and Lannan Awards. Carol Ann has also written extensively for children and has edited many anthologies. She is the Poet Laureate.

SAPPHO

Stung with Love: Poems and Fragments

Translated with an Introduction and Notes by
AARON POOCHIGIAN
and with a Preface by CAROL ANN DUFFY

PENGUIN BOOKS

PENGUIN CLASSICS

UK | USA | Canada | Ireland | Australia
India | New Zealand | South Africa

Penguin Books is part of the Penguin Random House group of companies
whose addresses can be found at global.penguinrandomhouse.com.

Penguin
Random House
UK

This translation first published in Penguin Classics 2009
Reprinted with two additional poems 2015

030

Selection, translation and editorial material copyright © Aaron Poochigian, 2009
Preface copyright © Carol Ann Duffy, 2009
All rights reserved

An extract from 'The Language of Women' by Rachel Hadas is reproduced on
page xxxii by kind permission of the author and of *The Hudson Review*, where it
first appeared in issue 60:4 (Winter 2008)

Set in 10.25/12.25 pt PostScript Adobe Sabon
Typeset by Rowland Phototypesetting Ltd, Bury St Edmunds, Suffolk
Printed in England by Clays Ltd, Elcograf S.p.A

ISBN: 978-0-140-45557-1

www.greenpenguin.co.uk

MIX
Paper from
responsible sources
FSC® C018179

Penguin Random House is committed to a
sustainable future for our business, our readers
and our planet. This book is made from Forest
Stewardship Council® certified paper.

Contents

Preface

She was born after 630 BC on the Greek island of Lesbos. Plato honoured her as the Tenth Muse, and she was to inspire the naming of both a sexuality and a poetics. The Ancient Greeks celebrated her as their finest poet and reproduced her image on their coins and vases, and poets from antiquity to the present day have recognized her supreme lyric gift. The Roman poets Catullus and Horace, who probably read her work in its entirety, emulated and were influenced by her. Horace declared in his *Odes* that her poems merited sacred admiration. The list of poets who have translated her, written versions of her poems or written poems about her, is endless, but includes Ovid, Sir Philip Sidney, John Donne, Alexander Pope, Byron, Coleridge, Tennyson, Thomas Hardy, Christina Rossetti, Amy Lowell, Edna St Vincent Millay, Ezra Pound and many poets writing in our own twenty-first century, notably the distinguished Canadian writer Anne Carson. Sappho's poems survive in fragments, some found as scrunched ingredients in papier mâché coffins, and in a handful of more complete lyrics; but ninety per cent of what she wrote is lost to us now. She would have sung her poems, accompanying herself on the lyre, and she may well have invented the *pēctis*, a variation of the instrument. It is from this ancient verse, sung to the lyre, that lyric poetry evolved. As one of a 'new wave' of Greek poets, she was one of the first poets to write out of the personal, moving away from the narrative of the gods to the direct and human story of the individual and in doing so she transformed the lyric line. In these wonderful new translations by Aaron Poochigian we hear the voice of a great and enduring poet in our ear again. Sappho.

Because once on a time you were
Young, sing of what is taking place,
Talk to us for a spell, confer
Your special grace.

Sappho's style was melodic, intimate, sensual, and she wrote
lyrics of love and desire, of loss and longing. As Poochigian
notes in his superb and meticulous introduction, there is always
something truly youthful about Sappho's spirit. She was a great
celebrator, had a poet's and a woman's eye for the 'gorgeous';
for flowers – chervil, rose, marigold and sweet clover; for smells
– frankincense, aniseed, myrrh and honey; she loved the moon
and 'The glitter and glamour of the sun'; she loved, as her
epithalamia, or marriage songs and other poems, show us, a
good party, a 'gleaming feast'. What is extraordinary, in reading
these startlingly fresh, new versions, is how much life is con-
veyed by so little. Presented with only a tenth of what she
wrote, we are vividly and deeply immersed in Sappho's world
– we walk with her on her island where 'the breeze feels as
gentle as honey' or where she sees an apple tree or hears a
nightingale singing the note of desire. And this is achieved
through a confident and shining poetic simplicity which has
endured for over two thousand years.

The greatest poets are able, long after their deaths, to speak
to our humanity and it is in her love poems that Sappho does
this most clearly. These poems are earned out of her openness
to desire, her willingness to love, her acceptance of a lover's
suffering. In this, too, her spirit is forever young. Her love
poems are why she endures and where we recognize ourselves:
infatuated and jealous; smitten and fulfilled; brain and tongue
shattered by love; wanting to die; remembering past encounters,
'all beautiful'. Aaron Poochigian's translations retain Sappho's
intense sense of being singingly alive and of being on the side
of youth, and loveliness, and love. They will find many new
readers for the major woman writer of antiquity.

Carol Ann Duffy

Chronology

Dates are birth–death for people.

after 630–c. 570 BCE Sappho.

c. 620–early to mid 500s BCE Alcaeus, a poet from Lesbos contemporary with Sappho, who may have composed the opening lines of 'I want to tell you something but good taste'.

384–322 BCE Aristotle, student of Plato and philosopher, whose *Rhetoric* preserves 'I want to tell you something but good taste'.

342–291 BCE Menander, writer of New Comedy, whose *Leucadia* recounts Sappho's legendary leap from the 'Shining Rock' (Leucas Petra).

c. 257–180 BCE Aristophanes of Byzantium, head librarian at the great library in Alexandria, who co-edits the nine-book collection of Sappho's poems with Aristarchus of Samothrace (*c.* 220–*c.* 143 BCE).

84–54 BCE Catullus, Roman poet, who adapts several of Sappho's poems, including 'That fellow strikes me as god's double'.

65–27 BCE Horace, Roman poet, who composes many of his *Odes* in the Sapphic stanza and describes Sappho's utterances as 'worthy of sacred awe' (*Ode* 2.13).

60–after 7 BCE Dionysius of Halicarnassus, Greek historian and rhetorician, whose *On Literary Composition* preserves Sappho's 'Subtly bedizened Aphrodite'.

43 BCE–17 CE Ovid, Roman poet, who popularizes the legend of Sappho's suicide in a literary epistle written in her voice (*Heroides* 15).

first century CE Longinus, Greek rhetorician and critic, whose *On the Sublime* preserves 'That fellow strikes me as god's double'.

125–185 CE Maximus of Tyre, Greek rhetorician and philosopher, whose *Orations* preserve, among other fragments, 'Here is the reason: it is wrong' and 'Like a gale smiting an oak'.

130–169 CE Hephaestion of Alexandria, Greek metrist, whose *Handbook on Metre* (an epitome of a longer work in 48 books) preserves numerous fragments of Sappho's poems, including 'A full moon shone' and 'Kytherea, precious'.

end of second–beginning of third century CE Athenaeus, Greek rhetorician and grammarian, whose lengthy *Scholars at Dinner* preserves numerous fragments, including 'The ambrosial mixture' and 'Once as a too, too lissome'.

331–363 CE Julian the Apostate, last polytheistic emperor of Rome, who cites Sappho's 'You were at hand' in a literary epistle addressed to the deceased Iamblicus (245–325 CE), a Syrian Neoplatonist philosopher.

end of tenth century CE The compilation of the *Suda*, a massive Byzantine encyclopedia containing a biographical entry on Sappho.

1110–80 CE John Tzetzes of Constantinople, Byzantine poet and grammarian, who laments that 'time has frittered away Sappho and her works, her lyre and songs' (*On the Metres of Pindar* 20–22).

Introduction

After his nephew had sung one of Sappho's songs over wine,
Solon of Athens, the son of Execestides, told the boy to teach
it to him at once. When someone asked Solon why he was so
eager, he answered, 'So that I may learn it and die.'

Aelian in Stobaeus 3.29.58

Born after 630 BCE, Sappho died around 570. She lived on
Lesbos, a large island in the Aegean near the coast of modern
Turkey. Lesbos was famous for the purity of its olive oil, as it
still is today, and for its wine, which Sappho's brother Charaxus
exported to Egypt. Though she may have been born in the
small town of Eresos, she spent most of her life in the largest
city on the island, Mytilene, an international emporium at the
crossroads between the Greek West and the Lydian East. Less
than a day's travel from the wealthy capital of the Lydian
Empire, Mytilene was renowned for luxury. According to
ancient report, the Lesbians themselves were luxury-loving, and
Sappho's poems present a mixture of Greek customs and exotic
Eastern commodities: she sings of ornate headbands and frank-
incense, and 'Lydian war cars at the ready' come to her mind
when she imagines a battle array.

We are given six different names for Sappho's father – the
one most often attested is Skamandrios, which at least has
the advantage of being derived from the Skamander River
in the Troad (north-western Turkey) near Lesbos. We hear of
three brothers: Eriguios, Larichos and Charaxus, the eldest.
The last, we assume, is the one mentioned in this fragment:

> Nereids, Kypris, please restore
> My brother to this port, unkilled.

During his voyages as a wine merchant to Naucratis (now Kom Ge'if in Egypt), Charaxus became involved with a courtesan named Doricha. Sappho is said to have reviled him for the entanglement but none of this invective has come down to us. Through we hear nothing of Eriguios, she did praise Larichos for obtaining the aristocratic office of cup-bearer at the town hall in Mytilene (this poem also has not survived).

Ancient and medieval biogaphies attest that Sappho had a daughter, Kleïs (Oxyrhynchus Papyrus 1800, fr. 1 and the *Suda* Σ 107). The conclusion was most likely drawn from this fragment:

> I have a daughter who reminds me of
> A marigold in bloom.
> Kleïs is her name,
> And I adore her.

The word *pais* which I have translated as 'daughter' can mean 'slave' as well as 'child' – thus we cannot determine whether Kleïs is the speaker's child or slave. Furthermore, we cannot be certain that the 'I' in this poem was expressing biographical details about the historical Sappho or even that the speaker was not some other character entirely. Some scholars, in fact, deny that Sappho had a daughter. In the tenth-century-CE Byzantine encyclopedia known as the *Suda* (or 'Stronghold'), the unidentified author of the entry on Sappho attests that her mother was also named Kleïs. Though he may simply have been operating under the assumption that grandmothers and granddaughters should have the same name, it is possible that he had access to more complete versions of the relevant fragments.

The *Suda* entry also claims that Sappho married 'a very rich man' but goes on to preserve, without a wink, a bawdy joke as the name of her husband: Kerikles (Prick) from the island of Andros (Man). It seems the claim that she had a husband is not to be taken seriously. It is attested that the poet Alcaeus (*c.* 620 – early to mid 500s BCE) was her lover but this inference probably resulted merely from the fact that they were contemporaries living on Lesbos. It is likely that they at least interacted, however, if Sappho did, in fact, compose the second part of 'I want to tell you something but good taste' as a response to one of Alcaeus' poems. Comic poets in the third century BCE name the poets Archilochus, Anacreon and Hipponax as her lovers, though the former lived a generation too early and the latter two a generation too late!

Other poets and playwrights include the Adonis-figure Phaon among Sappho's lovers. According to tradition, an old ferryman named Phaon once conveyed the goddess Aphrodite, disguised as an old woman, in his boat for free, and she repaid him by either transforming him into a beautiful youth or giving him 'an alabaster jar full of a lotion which he applied daily to make women fall in love with him' (Servius on Virgil's *Aeneid* 3.279). Sappho does show interest in the mythic affairs of goddesses with mortals – e.g. Aphrodite's affair with Adonis and Dawn's with Tithonous, and her allusions to these myths may explain how later readers came to assume that she herself had an affair with Phaon. The story that Sappho, in despair over her love for this irresistible youth, died by jumping from Leucas Petra (or the 'Shining Rock') into the Aegean probably derives from the fact that she mentions the rock in a poem. In a play by Menander (342–291 BCE) we find:

> They say that Sappho, while she was chasing haughty
>   Phaon,
> Was the first to throw herself, in her goading desire,
> From the rock that shines afar.
>
>   (*Leucadia* fr. 258)

This same 'Shining Rock' appears in Homer's *Odyssey* when the god Hermes escorts the souls of the suitors slain by Odysseus to the Underworld: 'and they passed by the streams of Okeanos and the Shining Rock and passed the Gates of the Sun and the District of Dreams' (24.11–12).[1] The rock came to be regarded as a kind of lover's leap that would cure the jumper of love one way or another, as death occasionally resulted. Though fitting for a poet of intense passions, both Sappho's love for a mythological character and her subsequent leap are, of course, unlikely to have been historical but are important for understanding the reception of Sappho in antiquity and modernity. The fatal leap provides a moral – the poet of love dies through an excess of passion, and her death serves to refute what she professed in her poetry. Furthermore, this uncontrollable heterosexual passion goes some way towards compensating for the homosexuality which made so many of Sappho's readers uncomfortable. Thus Ovid's *Heroides* 15 (written *c.* 15 BCE) presents Sappho as a reborn heterosexual who self-consciously states that her previous affections for various females do not compare with her love for Phaon.

In a philosophical dialogue by Plato (428/7–348/7 BCE) Socrates, a character in it, calls Sappho 'beautiful' (*Phaedrus* 235b). Writing five hundred years later, Maximus of Tyre (125–185 CE) explains that this adjective must have been intended to refer to her poetry because Sappho 'was repugnant and exceedingly ugly, being dark in complexion and rather short' (*Orations* 18.7). This description may result simply from a biographer's assumptions concerning her interest in women. We have no contemporary accounts of her appearance, and no coins or statues bearing her image appear until centuries after her death. It is safer to leave Sappho's physical appearance a mystery.

We receive no specific information about the daily operation of the group of females associated with Sappho, only assertions that she kept a 'school'. Evidence from the songs and later testimony confirms that this group consisted primarily of girls between the ages of puberty and marriage. The *Suda* biography lists her female love-interests as 'companions and friends' with whom 'she had a disgraceful friendship': Atthis, Telesippa and Megara. The same source also assigns her the 'disciples' Anagora, Gongyla and Eunica. All these names seem simply to have been gleaned from the poems, and their relationships to Sappho determined partly by the context in which they appeared and partly by the biographer's imagination. We are told that she had 'rivals' as well, Andromeda and Gorgo, and subsequent tradition has made these women into headmistresses for competing schools. Modern scholarship has widely disagreed over the nature of Sappho's group: some scholars accept the traditional 'school' interpretation; others regard the group as a religious organization or a club analogous to contemporary male *hetaireiai* (or political clubs) on Lesbos. In order to determine, as best as we can, the nature of her group, it will be useful to take a look at society on Lesbos during her lifetime.

Sappho in Context

Throughout the Hellenic world the seventh and sixth centuries BCE were a time of transition from inherited kingships, such as Homer describes in the *Iliad* and *Odyssey*, to a world in which tyranny, oligarchy and eventually democracy were viable alternatives. The Archaic Greek world (seventh–mid-fifth centuries BCE) remained the 'agonistic' (or competitive) society which we encounter in Homer, with honour (*timē*) as the commodity of highest value. However, with the rise of the polis (or city-state) we find a proliferation of the unconstitutional dictators called 'tyrants'. The period named after them, the Age of Tyrants, is characterized by conflicts between these rulers and the general population, on the one hand, and aristocrats (the class to which most Archaic Greek poets belonged), on the other.

For several centuries before Sappho's time, a family-clan called the Penthelids ruled Mytilene. Like many royal families, the Penthelids claimed descent from a legendary founder, and their patriarch, Penthilus, was said to be the illegitimate son of two mythic figures, Orestes and Ergane, daughter of Aegisthus. According to legend, Penthilus led the Aeolian migration from central and northern Greece (Boeotia and southern Thrace) to Lesbos. The Penthelids were pre-eminent among other noble families on Lesbos through the eighth century BCE, and only they and other arms-bearing landholders counted as citizens. Their government was essentially a monarchy, though the king would meet with the nobles out of courtesy before presenting his policies. Our earliest sources depict the seventh-century

Penthelids as cruel – 'going about striking people with clubs' (Aristotle, *Politics* 1311b26). Like other tyrants of the period, this family seems to have surrounded itself with a bodyguard of club-bearers. There are several possible reasons for these security measures: the seventh century saw the colonial expansion of Lesbos, military campaigns in the Troad (the area around Troy) and greater mercantile activity. The aristocrats became wealthy from these activities and most likely chafed under the Penthelids' rule. On two occasions during the century leaders of aristocratic factions attempted to overthrow the monarchy: first, Megacles 'with his friends' rushed the Penthelids but, though he killed many of them, the clan remained in power (Aristotle, *Politics* 1311b26, b29). Subsequently Smardis killed the last Penthelid king, aptly named after his family's legendary forebear. This assassination did lead to a change in government, though Smardis, according to Aristotle, acted only to avenge his wife's rape. We hear little of the Penthelids in the sixth century, and it seems that they became merely one among a number of rival clans.

The other aristocratic families subsequently competed for supremacy and no stable government emerged. *Hetaireiai* contributed to the divisiveness on Mytilene, in that they promoted loyalty to clan (fathers, brothers, uncles and more distant family) over the state. The songs of Alcaeus provide vivid glimpses into his *hetaireia*. We find him praising ancestral deeds and weapons and galvanizing political views. Sappho also clearly belonged to an aristocratic family: she had access to luxury items and education, she seems to have shared some of Alcaeus' political views, and her brothers held an honorary government post and exported wine.

To put an end to strife between these clans, Melanchrus, a noble himself, was set up in 612 BCE to rule in the same manner as the Penthelid kings. He became the first 'tyrant' of Mytilene, though it should be pointed out that 'tyrant' is not necessarily pejorative at this time – it simply means a king who came to the throne by other than hereditary means. A number of noble families, including that of Alcaeus, conspired to kill Melanchrus and selected Pittacus (*c.* 640–568 BCE) as tyrant-killer. The plot was successful, and the government then reverted to clan-strife. There was no immediate conflict, however, because many nobles soon left Mytilene to campaign against the Athenians in the Sigean War (608 BCE).

The Athenians had contested the Lesbian claim to the Troad (the region where the legendary city of Troy, now Hissarlik, was located). When the Athenians were about to attack Mytilene, Pittacus challenged their general Phrynon to single combat, with the understanding that the result should decide the war. Pittacus won but, though again the hero, did not seize absolute power. A nobleman Myrsilus was appointed the second tyrant of Mytilene instead. Alcaeus describes Myrsilus' rise to power as a 'wave again, greater than before' (fr. 6.1–2), and Sappho herself refers, with some disapproval, to Myrsilus' family in a patchy fragment (fr. 98b.7).[2] Alcaeus' family, again in association with Pittacus, conspired to overthrow this second tyrant. At the last moment, however, Pittacus backed out, and the plot failed. He then rose to a position of second-in-command under Myrsilus, and the nobles involved in the plot went into exile in the backcountry of Lesbos. Alcaeus presents a pitiable image of himself during his first exile:

> The property which my father
> And father's father grew old possessing
> Amid citizens always killing each other
> – from this I have been driven, an exile
> Beyond the hinterland. Like Onomakles,
> I settled here alone in the wolf-thickets.
>   (fr. 130b, 5–10)

During the tyranny of Myrsilus Sappho may have had to go into exile in Sicily, possibly because her family was involved in the plot. In a tattered fragment that refers obscurely to 'exile' Sappho seems, for a time, to be cut off from luxuries and utters a frustrated complaint to Kleïs (most likely her daughter):

> I do not have an
> Ornately woven
> Bandeau to hand you,
> Kleïs. From
> Where would it come?

The Roman orator Cicero (102–43 BCE) mentions a statue of Sappho in the town hall at Syracuse on Sicily but there is no way to determine whether her visit there occasioned a memorial (*Against Verres* 2.4.125). Both the dates and the very occurrence of Sappho's exile are contested.

When Myrsilus died *c.* 597 BCE, the exiled nobles returned to Mytilene and celebrated, but Pittacus sought to gain further legitimacy among the Lesbian nobility by taking a wife from the Penthelids. Though Sappho's poems do not comment directly on this union, a patchy fragment does refer, with contempt, to a Mika's affiliation with this family: 'I will not allow you . . . you opted for the friendship of the daughters of the Penthelids . . . you of bad character' (fr. 71.2–4). Pittacus then drove his worst enemies again into exile (Alcaeus' clan among them) and ruled Mytilene as *aesymnētēs* (or ruler) for ten years until he resigned in 585 BCE. He passed laws discouraging debauchery and other sumptuary laws aimed at aristocrats, including restrictions on funeral expenditure. For all the invective levelled against him in the songs of Alcaeus, Pittacus came to be regarded as one of the Seven Sages of Greece.

Social Context and Sappho's Group

As we have seen, evidence from the poems and later testimony suggests that Sappho was an aristocrat who had a position of leadership over a group consisting of females, most of whom were in a state of premarital adolescence. She addresses females familiarly and affectionately in the plural as *korai* (girls), *paides* (children or girls) and *parthenoi* (maidens). *Parthenoi* specifically indicates adolescent females in the age group between puberty and marriage. On occasion Sappho addresses these girls as *hetairai* (companions or fellow group-members). *Hetaira* in male discourse comes to mean not just 'female companion' but 'prostitute', and it is likely that the predominance of this second sense contributed to the tradition that Sappho was herself a prostitute.

The nature of Sappho's all-female group is a vexed and contentious issue. Scholars have presented a number of competing theories: Sappho as schoolmistress, a performer at symposia and even a leader of a *thiasos* (religious community). Since there is evidence both in favour of and against each of these theories, it will be helpful to review them briefly before arriving at a general conclusion.

The School

Numerous ancient sources attest that Sappho was a teacher of young women, and the great German nineteenth-century scholar Ulrich von Wilamowitz-Moellendorf, on the basis of this evidence, argued that Sappho was headmistress of a *Mädchenpensionat*, or boarding school for girls, which operated along the lines of nineteenth-century boarding schools. In an attempt to lay this interpretation to rest, Holt Parker contends that 'nowhere in any poem does Sappho teach, or speak about teaching, anything to anyone',[3] but this is true only in terms of formal education as we understand it today. One of Sappho's predecessors, the epic poet Homer, was regarded as first and foremost among poet–teachers and, it was alleged, could provide a complete education in himself. Homeric education consisted simply of hearing and memorizing excerpts from his epics – there was no set curriculum involving reading, writing and arithmetic. We do not find 'schools' as we understand them until late-fifth-century Athens, and it is in this period that the comic poet Aristophanes, aware of the change, caricatures the outdated style of education: his Stronger Argument, a character in the *Clouds*, explains that the old education consisted primarily of memorizing traditional poetry and 'intoning the musical modes [the students'] fathers passed down to them' (966–72). No doubt Sappho was not running a boarding school for girls in the early sixth century BCE in just the way that modern scholars might imagine.

Like the other Archaic poets, however, Sappho does pass on advice. We find the most obvious examples in gnomic statements, that is, traditional wisdom pithily expressed so as to be remembered and handed down. Such expressions in Sappho are as didactic as similar statements in Hesiod's practical manual for farmers, the *Works and Days* (*c.* 700 BCE). Take the following example:

> Wealth without real worthiness
> Is no good for the neighbourhood;
> But their proper mixture is
> The summit of beatitude.

In a largely preliterate culture, formal education as we understand it did not exist, and much instruction consisted of just such pithy, memorable statements.

As part of her duties as poet Sappho would have trained choruses to perform her choral songs. Though it is difficult in many instances to determine which songs were performed by a chorus, the epithalamia (or wedding songs) have been accepted as choral since antiquity, and the composition of public songs, including epithalamia, would have entailed the training of the chorus and probably the participation of the singer and/or accompanist at the performance. Several fragments suggest that Sappho also instructed girls in monodic (or solo) song. For example, in one we find a speaker exhorting another female to 'please pick up [her] lyre, / Praise Gongyla'. Musical training would have comprised much of Archaic Greek education for the elite, and another fragment specifically names a *Moisopolōn domos* ('House of Those Dedicated to the Muses' or maybe even 'Conservatory'):

> Here is the reason: it is wrong
> To play a funeral song
> In the Musicians' House –
> It simply would not be decorous.

Though again it is difficult to be certain, 'the Musicians' House' was most likely an institution which provided training in choral and monodic song, if not other arts as well.

Anne Burnett argues that Sappho's songs were educational in a more general sense, in that 'an older woman taught [girls] what it was to be a girl, that they might better become women later on'.[4] Thus the speaker of one fragment invites an older woman to teach a community of girls 'just what to do' at a wedding ceremony:

> Because once on a time you were
> Young, sing of what is taking place,
> Talk to us for a spell, confer
> Your special grace.
>
> For we march to a wedding – yes,
> You know it well.

In the face of this evidence, Martin West's summation of the issue is inevitable: 'later writers saw [Sappho] as a chorus-leader or teacher . . . We cannot tell how accurate a construction this is, but it must have been based on the impression given by the poems, and it is consistent with what we know.'[5] Whatever the nature of her group, we can be confident that Sappho passed on proverbial wisdom and instructed girls in choral and probably monodic song. She would no doubt have been very influential on females, especially during their post-pubescent and pre-marital years. Sappho's 'school' may have been as informal a gathering as the group of young men around Socrates in Athens in the late fifth century BCE. If we must speak of a 'school' at all, it more resembled a finishing school and conservatory than a boarding school.

The Symposium and the Hetaireia

Drawing on parallels in the poems of Alcaeus and Anacreon, Parker argues that Sappho performed her songs at aristocratic drinking parties called symposia.[6] Solo performance was standard at symposia as at *hetaireiai*, which were, in essence, politically oriented symposia. Parker's thesis is most revolutionary in its claim that Sappho sang of her love not for girls but for other adult women at all-female symposia. Since there is no evidence to corroborate female symposia and *hetaireiai* and since many of Sappho's songs were clearly written for choral rather than monodic performance, this view is untenable. All the same, as Burnett explains, '[Sappho's] circle, like the *hetaireia*, had a customary role to play in Lesbian society, and it too was aristocratic, musical and constrained only by bonds of love and loyalty.'[7] Furthermore, with its clear-cut boundaries dividing the included from the excluded, Sappho's group served a social function similar to that of a *hetaireia*.

Hetaireiai coalesced the values which those included in the group shared and ridiculed those who lacked them. Thus, Alcaeus composed a song for his that 'focused upon much loved objects and reminded his audience of the solidarity of his band of exiled nobles, the purpose which united them against external forces'.[8] Alcaeus' definitive list consists of weapons associated with famous battles in which his forebears had played a part:

> The whole ceiling has been fitted out for the war-god:
> Bright helmets, from which white horse-hair crests
> Nod to us, decorations for the heads of men;
> Gleaming bronze greaves [shin armor] on hidden pegs,
> Ramparts to stout arrows; fresh linen corselets,
> And hollow shields set down on the floor ...
> We have not been able to forget these things
> Since we first took up this task.
>
> (fr. 140)

Sappho provides similar litanies, but hers consist of decorative items:

> With sweet red garments, bracelets made of gold,
> Beautiful baubles, ivory and untold
> Chalices chased in silver.

This taste for finery set standards of dress and appearance. We frequently encounter floral accessories and perfumes (e.g. 'lavish infusions in queenly quantities') in her songs, and these beautiful objects and exotic scents clearly had importance for those who wore and admired them. The fragments that linger over details of toilette and fashion imply membership in an exclusive group – the *kalai* (the 'gorgeous ones') who presented themselves in the accepted manner:

> As for you girls, the gorgeous (*kalai*) ones,
> There will be no change in my plans.

Sappho's frequent disapproval of outré taste further underscores the importance of luxuries to her group. We hear of a number of rivals, and the names Andromeda and Gorgo, in particular, recur both as threats and objects of ridicule. The name 'Gorgo' may well be a derisive nickname (it means 'Gorgon'), and Andromeda, we are told, is the rustic female mocked thus:

> What farm girl, garbed in fashions from the farm
> And witless of the way
> A hiked hem would display
> Her ankles, captivates you with her charm?

It is striking that the déclassée Andromeda is criticized here not for being too free with her favours but for *not* knowing how to present herself in an enticing manner. At least one criterion for inclusion in this group was dressing attractively or, as Burnett puts it, giving 'a sign that one was ready to please'.[9] In the end, though there is no evidence that Sappho's group was politically oriented and though it was certainly not a *hetaireia* like Alcaeus' all-male club, it operated socially along similar lines, using status symbols to define inclusion and songs to express its values.

Thiasos (or Religious Community)

We have seen evidence that Sappho's group involved the cultivation of girls in preparation for marriage and that musical training was part of this preparation. One theory takes this a step further, arguing that Sappho's group was a *thiasos* that provided an officially sanctioned rite of passage for adolescent females, but it is difficult to confirm given the absence of contemporary Lesbian evidence for female *thiasoi* beyond the hints in Sappho's poems.

Scholars often cite as a parallel the Spartan public upbringing called the *agōgē* in which boys and girls separately participated. It is probable that the *agōgē* for girls began in Archaic times and that the Spartan institution was therefore contemporary with Sappho's group. Whereas participation in the *agōgē* was obligatory for the daughters of citizens, membership in Sappho's circle seems to have been voluntary and even international – that is, if her 'disciples' Anagora and Gongyla did, in fact, come to Mytilene from Miletus and Colophon. Furthermore, since Spartan girls lived at home during the *agōgē*, they were not separated from their families as they were going through the initiation process. Claude Calame, the leading proponent of the *thiasos* theory, reads the terms *adikein* ('to commit an injustice') and *philotes* ('love based on mutual confidence') in 'Subtly bedizened Aphrodite' as evidence supporting an institutional base for Sappho's group: 'To betray Sappho was not only to betray the intimate reciprocal relationship of *philia* [mutual love] the poetess was setting up with the girls of her group, but it meant also to break the bonds sanctioned by a contract.'[10] According to Calame, the group provided post-pubescent, unmarried girls with an environment regulated by rules and with activities such as musical training.

Evidence from Sparta also provides evidence for homoerotic attachments like those portrayed in Sappho's poems. In a discussion of Spartan pederasty, Plutarch explains that 'this sort of love was so esteemed among them that fair and noble women also loved maidens' (*Life of Lycurgus* 18.4). The Spartan poet Alcman's First and Third *Patheneia* ('Maiden Songs', late seventh century BCE) provide evidence of socially sanctioned homoerotic attachments. In the First a chorus of maidens expresses admiration for the awe-striking beauty of its chorus leaders, Agido and Hagesichora. In the Third the chorus looks on Astymeloisa's beauty with 'limb-loosening desire' (61). It is striking that, within this socially sanctioned context, homo-erotic expression became a standard theme in public song. Sappho and her girls express similar admiration for members of their sex and sometimes even use similar images. When writing in the first person Sappho expresses a lover's passion towards other females, and, as Calame observes, it is difficult to deny 'that the fragments evoking the power of Eros, to mention only these, refer to a real love that was physically consum-mated'.[11] Sappho's public profession of homosexuality in song, in a sense, provides further support for a socially and religiously sanctioned basis for her group, since, as Chris Bennett explains, 'Sappho's feelings could not have been expressed openly unless it had been socially sanctioned, nor socially sanctioned unless religiously sanctioned.'[12] There was no local evidence to corrob-orate the all-female milieu presented in many of Sappho's poems until 1995 when the Polyxena Sarcophagus, dated to 525–500 BCE, was excavated from a tomb in the Northern Troad. One long side of the sarcophagus represents females in an intimate setting: one holds a mirror, while another pats a third affection-ately on the back. Though this scene is not erotic, we can at least be certain that Sappho's intimate female group had a nearby and roughly contemporary parallel.

To determine whether Sappho's group was a *thiasos* we must determine whether it was religious or secular in nature. We find invocations of numerous female deities in Sappho's poems: Aphrodite, Hera, the Muses, the Graces and the Nereids. While reading the extant fragments, one gets the sense that Sappho is giving Greek mythology a feminine slant. Though Zeus is the 'father of gods and men' and the most important of the Olympian deities, he is never an addressee of prayers and is mentioned only in relation to his daughters, Aphrodite, Artemis, the Graces and the Muses. The virgin goddess Artemis appears in one narrative fragment ('Artemis made the pledge no god can break') but is never invoked. Athena, another virgin goddess and perhaps the most prominent deity in Homer's *Iliad* and *Odyssey*, is never mentioned in Sappho. Apollo (as Paeon) and Hermes appear once, and each time in a publicly oriented and Homericizing fragment. Eros, son of Aphrodite, is the most prominent male divinity. Even with numerous invocations of female divinities, however, it is difficult to determine whether Sappho's hymns were religious in nature or intended only as performance pieces. Writing in the 1950s, Denys Page argues that her hymns must be 'records of personal experience, designed to be heard rather by mortals than gods, to be judged by the standards not of priesthood but of poetry'.[13] Page's conclusion most likely results from discomfort with the way that Sappho mingles the religious and the erotic. The assumption that these elements cannot coexist, however, is based on a misconception of the jurisdiction of Aphrodite. Surely Aphrodite Pandemos ('of all the people'), who was responsible for lower sexual life and in particular for prostitution, received hymnal entreaties far more explicit than what we find in Sappho. In short, erotic images and situations do not preclude a song from being a sincere address to Aphrodite. 'Leave Crete and sweep to this blest temple', for example, simultaneously presents a cult setting and 'an extended and multiperspective metaphor for women's sexuality'.[14] In contrast to Page, Walter Burkert asserts that 'the worship of Aphrodite finds its most personal and most complete expression in the poems of Sappho'.[15]

Sappho frequently uses formal hymnal structure. 'Subtly bedizened Aphrodite' breaks down into the tripartite structure of a traditional kletic hymn (or hymn that summons a god): invocation and summons (1–5), *hypomnēsia* or citation of previous requests and the god's past deeds (5–24) and entreaty (25–8). Another hymn, which, as far as we can tell, was not erotic, also adheres closely to this structure:

> Reveal your graceful figure here,
> Close to me, Hera. I make entreaty
> Just as the kings once made their prayer,
> The famous Atreidai –

> Winning victories by the score
> At Troy first, then at sea, they sailed
> The channel to this very shore,
> Tried leaving but failed
>
> Until they prayed to you, the Saviour
> Zeus and Thyone's charming son.
> Like long ago, then, grant this favour,
> As you have done . . .

Nothing in this hymn suggests that it is not sincere. Furthermore, even the erotic hymns are not in any way subversive – they are often striking but never shocking. To make this distinction clear, we need only consider Madonna's 'Like a Prayer' (1989), a pop song that also mingles the religious and the erotic. The lyrics, which at one point seem simultaneously to evoke genuflection and fellatio, could be interpreted as intended to shock the devout. Sappho's erotic hymns, in contrast, do not have a sharp ironic edge. Though, like Aphrodite in Sappho's most famous hymn, they smile on occasion, they never sneer. If the hymns are subversive, they are so in subtler ways. In the end, though at least some of the hymns are genuine addresses to deities, we cannot be certain that her group had a religious affiliation. Even if it did not, however, Sappho's poems make clear that certain deities were important in the circle's everyday life.

Though we cannot with certainty identify Sappho's group as a *thiasos*, the literary evidence from Sparta and material evidence from Hellenized Asia corroborate the impressions created by her fragments: the group consisted exclusively of females and involved an (official or unofficial) rite of passage that began after puberty and ended with social integration through marriage. Operating as a discrete social organism, the group had a strong sense of what sorts of taste and behaviour marked it as special. Furthermore, Sappho and a chorus of girls, on occasion, sang genuinely religious hymns and performed songs in public. As these performances required training, Sappho instructed the girls in voice and music, and the songs which the girls learned provided further instruction through role models in the same way as characters in Homeric epic did for males. All of this training served to ease the transition from adolescent to married life and make the girls more attractive as brides.

Epithalamia

Sappho's epithalamia and Alcaeus' mythic 'Marriage of Peleus and Thetis' comprise the entirety of our evidence for wedding rituals in Lesbos in the late seventh/early sixth centuries BCE. Though practices would have varied from region to region and through time, it will be helpful to provide a general outline of Ancient Greek wedding rituals based on these poems and on comparative evidence.

In fifth-century Athens the engagement ceremony, called *engeuēsis*, involved a legally binding agreement between the bride's *kyrios* (or legal guardian), who was usually her father, and the groom. At this time, the dowry was agreed upon, and oaths were sworn in front of witnesses. The bride usually was not present, and the groom often did not see the bride until her unveiling on the day of the wedding. In a famous monologue in which she argues that women are 'the most abused creatures of all', the mythic Medea complains of the bride's powerlessness in this situation: 'we bid a very high price in dowries only to buy a man to be master of our bodies ... then comes the greatest risk: will we end up with a good man or a bad?' (Euripides, *Medea* 231–5). Sappho makes no mention of this ceremony other than the extravagant dowry which Andromache brings with her to Troy. The epithalamia of hers we possess belong to the next stage.

The wedding ceremony proper, called the *ekdosis*, involved the 'giving away' of the bride to her new *kyrios*, the groom. A banquet was held at the father of the bride's house which included male and female kin and members of the community. Here offerings were made to the gods and wedding hymns were sung. Next, a wedding procession singing ritualized and bawdy songs transferred the bride to the house of the groom.

'Carpenters, raise the rafter-beam' most likely was performed at the banquet, as it describes the arrival of the groom separately from that of the bride:

> Carpenters, raise the rafter-beam
> (For Hymen's wedding hymn)
> A little higher to make room
> (For Hymen's wedding hymn)
> Because here comes the groom –
> An Ares more imposing than
> A giant, a terribly big man.

The groom is 'terribly big' here not only because of his pride but because his penis, we are to infer, is fantastically erect. Here we first encounter the bawdy humour which appears in many of the epithalamia. Sappho provides us with a glorified portrayal of the wedding-procession in 'Idaos, then, the panting emissary':

> ... And sweetly then the double-oboe's cadence
> Mingled with rhythmic rattles as the maidens
> Sang sacred songs. A fine sound strode the air.
> Cups on the roadside, vessels everywhere,
> Cassia and frankincense were mixed with myrrh.
> Old women (venerable as they were)
> Warbled and trilled. The men all in a choir
> Summoned first that lover of the lyre,
> The long-range archer, Paeon, then extolled
> Andromache and Hector, godlike to behold.

Upon arriving at the groom's house, the bride and groom went straight to the bridal chamber (*thalamos*) where for the first time the bride removed her veil. This unveiling (or *anaka-lyptēria*) was in many instances the first time that the groom saw the bride. We also have clear evidence for the removal of a 'bridal belt' (*zōma, zōnē* in Classical Greek) in Lesbian wedding ritual. Henceforth the bride and groom were considered married. Outside the bridal chamber while the bride and groom consummated their union, loud wedding songs were sung to scare away evil spirits. Giulia Sissa argues that they also served 'to cover the cry that [the bride] will emit in the midst of her first embrace'.[16] The following fragment was most likely sung outside of the marriage chamber:

> And may the maidens all night long
> Celebrate your shared love in song
> And the bride's bosom,
> A violet-blossom.
>
> Get up, now! Rouse that gang of fellows –
> Your boys – and we shall sleep as well as
> The bird that intones
> Piercing moans.

In addition to the songs sung before the chamber door, one groomsman was customarily appointed 'doorkeeper'. When the bride's friends staged a ritual attempt to 'save' the bride, he would repel them. In the following fragment, the doorkeeper's feet are broad both so that he can better guard the door and so that the chorus can hint that he has an enormous penis:

> It would take seven fathoms to span
> The feet of the doorkeeper (the best man);
> His sandals are five cows' worth of leather
> And ten shoemakers stitched them together.

True to her duties as public poet, Sappho presents only moments of joy in the festal epithalamia, though, inevitably, the process must often have been traumatic for the bride. Lyn Wilson observes that, for 'the young woman moving from the safety of her parent's house or the sensual, female environment of the Sapphic community, the experience is perhaps more ambivalent than this unqualified festivity would suggest'.[17]

Style

Until very recently Sappho's longest and best-preserved songs all had to do with erotic situations. With the discovery of a fragment in the Cologne University Archives in 2004, we acquired a new, nearly complete song, 'Girls, chase the violet-bosomed Muses' bright', in which the singer laments old age rather than frustrated love. In fact, a minority of Sappho's songs are erotic. A survey reveals a remarkable range and versatility: Sappho narrates epic events in a Homeric style as well as recounts what presents itself as intense personal experience in a distinctive voice. We at times admire 'the uncommon objectivity of her demeanor towards her own extremity' and at others appreciate a radical subjectivity which can envisage comparisons such as 'more golden than gold' (fr. 156.2).[18]

Scholars often comment on Sappho's ability to activate multiple perspectives within the same poem and to elide differences between subject and object. The singer of 'Abanthis, please pick up your lyre', for example, exhorts Abanthis to sing of her affection for Gongyla, thereby drawing attention to her own act of singing. This singer goes on to state that, when she notices Abanthis is aroused by Gongyla's attire, she is herself 'in ecstasy'. The singer thus identifies herself with Abanthis (who is herself a singer) and feels excitement for a second absent girl through her own identification with the first. As part of this process, the singer strives to make herself more appealing to Abanthis, and the two characters are both subjects who feel desire and objects which rouse it – they are mutually lover and beloved. Feminist scholars have pointed out that, in contrast to the power-dynamic common in masculine erotic encounters, the singer 'does not attempt to impose her will upon the person she loves but instead, through engaging appeals, tries to elicit a corresponding response from her'.[19]

We can partly attribute Sappho's ability to bring multiple perspectives into play to the variety of roles she was obliged to play in life: she was a female who engaged with a male-dominated poetic tradition and performed in a male-centric society. She exhibits double consciousness – a simultaneous awareness of the traditional male-authorized view and of her own distinctly feminine 'take'. Jack Winkler explains that double consciousness develops naturally in women in a male-prominent society, who are 'like a linguistic minority in a culture whose public actions are all conducted in the majority language. To participate even passively in the public arena the minority must be bilingual; the majority feels no such need to learn the minority's language.'[20] A contemporary poet, Rachel Hadas, succinctly describes the nature of this polyglottal feminine discourse in *The Language of Women*:

> But women's lives are fissured and to show it
> A multitasking tongue is what we need . . .
>
> we women know
> at least two modes of speech and maybe three:
> the public and the private, high and low.[21]

The poems which interact with and reinterpret Homer best exhibit Sappho's double consciousness. In 'Subtly bedizened Aphrodite', for example, Sappho evokes Homeric divine machinery for what is ostensibly a personal matter: the named 'Sappho' in the poem begins her hymn in much the same manner as Diomedes in Book 5 of the *Iliad*. Aphrodite then comes to Sappho in a chariot drawn by swallows just as Hera and Athena descend to Diomedes in a war chariot drawn by flying horses. To drive this extended allusion to the *Iliad* home, Sappho entreats Aphrodite to be her *summachos* ('ally in battle') in the final stanza. Speaking of this appropriation of Homeric images and situations, Mary Lefkowitz observes that 'it is as if Sappho were saying that what happens in a woman's life also partakes of the significance of the man's world of war'.[22] In a tragedy written a century and a half later, Medea makes a similar challenge:

> Men allege that we live safe and sound at home
> While they must go to war with their spears.
> They are so stupid! I would rather stand there

> Three times in battle holding my shield up
> Than give birth once.
>
> (Euripides, *Medea*, 148–51)

Like Euripides' Medea, Sappho uses military images and diction to elevate the events of female life to a level equal with those of a male's. Furthermore, rather than presenting women simply as objects of desire, Sappho presents us with female characters who act autonomously. In 'Some call ships, infantry or horsemen' Helen of Troy, the object of desire par excellence, gives up her husband and family of her own free will for the thing that she desires – Paris. Page Dubois sees in this poem 'one of the few texts which break the silence of women in antiquity, an instant in which women become more than the objects of man's desire'.[23]

A refined taste for pretty things, both artificial and natural, characterizes Sappho's songs, and such delights, as mentioned above, served to define the values of her aristocratic circle. In 'Idaos, then, the panting emissary' we find a distinctly Sapphic description of the dowry. The richness of the gifts has been compressed into as little metrical space as possible so that the items seem to merge in a single mass. In many fragments flowers appear, both growing in the wild and culled as material for garlands and necklaces. Eva Stehle Stigers observes that, as a general rule, flowers in Sappho symbolize a 'fragile combination of opposites' consisting of 'intimacy and distance, eroticism and innocence'.[24] Thus the roses and wild flowers in 'Leave Crete and sweep to this blest temple' contribute to an erotic landscape that is simultaneously an inviolable sacred space and a pleasure garden where Aphrodite will abound. In 'Off in Sardis' the singer uses an image of flowers in the moonlight to bridge the distance between a girl in Lydia and the present locale where she is addressing the absent girl's beloved Atthis:

> Dew is poured out in handsome fashion; lissome
> Chervil unfurls; Rose
> And Sweet Clover with heady flowers blossom.

The flowers respond to the moonlight as the singer and Atthis respond to the absent girl's beauty, and the moonlight which opens the flowers bridges the distance by creating the same private world for the three of them.

There is evidence that Sappho incorporated these pretty things into a sort of aesthetic credo. Athenaeus claims that she 'did not separate *to kalon* (the beautiful) from *habrotēs* (extravagance)' (*Scholars at Dinner* 15.687a). The following best expresses the sublimation of *habrotēs* into something greater:

> But I love extravagance,
> And wanting it has handed down
> The glitter and glamour of the sun
> As my inheritance.

An appreciation for luxury has led to an abstract quality, 'the beautiful' itself perhaps, symbolized here by the 'glitter and glamour of the sun'. In one very short fragment ('more golden than gold', fr. 156.2) a comparison involving a luxury paradoxically points to something that surpasses the luxury in its own quality, most likely the appearance of a girl. Burnett explains the relationship between extravagance and beauty as part of a 'circular, Sapphic law according to which beauty demands love and love, in turn, creates the beautiful'.[25] Sappho's frequent use of *eraton* (lovely), an adjective which expresses both desire and loveliness, embodies this symbiosis. Her songs, then, begin with a love for the beautiful which, in turn, generates even more beauty.

Sappho's style is deceptively simple. The sentence structure is most often paratactic, that is, sentences occur one after the other without subordinating clauses, like beads on a string. This style serves her well in 'Idaos, then, the panting emissary' in which she relates a sequence of events: sentence by sentence, the glory (*kleos*) of Andromache's arrival at Troy spreads from the messenger's mouth to King Priam's ear and from there to the entire community. This style is also effective for representing simultaneous symptoms of love, such as speechlessness, fever and blurred vision in 'That fellow strikes me as god's double'. Both in modernity and in antiquity Sappho's songs have been admired for their sonic richness. Dionysius of Halicarnassus (60–after 7 BCE) cites Sappho's poetry as an example of the 'elegant style' which 'judges which collocations will make the music more melodious, and assesses by what arrangements the words will result in more pleasing combinations, and thus it strives to fit each word in place, taking care to have everything planned and rubbed smooth and all the junctures neatly fitted' (*Demosthenes* 40). Charles Segal takes this sonic richness a step further, arguing that Sappho's language is incantatory and its effect is *thelxis* (enchantment): '. . . for Sappho the "power" of love is a god, as power often is for the ancient Greeks, and as such is to be summoned before her by the incantatory power and the quasi-magical *thelxis* of her poetry. Her poetry both portrays *thelxis* and, in a sense, *is thelxis*.'[26] The fragments do resonate a dense, voluptuous texture of sound. The sounds and rhythms of poetry serve, in general, to distinguish poetry from everyday speech. Sappho, however, uses them not merely for this purpose but also, in effect, to draw a magic circle around her songs.

Performance Context

Scholars have traditionally maintained a canonical distinction between choral poets, whose compositions were performed publicly by singer-dancers, and monodic poets who performed solo to the accompaniment of the lyre. Pindar (522–443 BCE) and Bacchylides (fifth century BCE), as authors of publicly performed victory odes, were assigned to the former class, and other 'lyric' poets, including Sappho, to the latter. Monodic poetry was held to express 'personal' sentiment whereas choral poetry expressed 'public' sentiment. The lyre is indeed an inextricable attribute of Sapphic iconography: she mentions and addresses them, she is credited with the invention of the *pēctis* (large many-stringed lyre) and the *plectrum* (pick for a lyre), and artists both in antiquity and modernity most often represent her with lyre in hand.

All the same, scholarship has called this polarizing distinction between choral and monodic poets into question. In the *Partheneia* of Alcman a chorus of girls expresses 'personal' sentiments traditionally regarded as typical of monodic song. The question then arises: if choruses express personal sentiment in Alcman, were any of the equally 'personal' songs of Sappho also performed by a chorus? André Lardinois sums up the 'personality' debate thus: 'can we be sure that any of the early Greek poems is "personal" . . . ? What is "personality" in such a group-oriented society as archaic Greece? Central to the debate [over "personality" in Archaic poetry] have been poems in which the poet clearly impersonates a character. Some of these we find, interestingly enough, among Sappho's fragments as well.'[27] Lardinois's studies have established that, for most of Sappho's songs, there is more evidence in support of choral performance than monodic. The epithalamia have been accepted as choral since antiquity, and these songs were sung during the wedding ceremony by age-mates of the bride. Ancient sources also claim that Sappho wrote cult hymns. Of the remaining poems, 'Kytherea, precious' provides the strongest evidence for choral performance – it is clearly antiphonal. A chorus of girls asks Aphrodite:

> 'Kytherea, precious
> Adonis is nearly dead.
> How should we proceed?'

A singer impersonating Aphrodite responds:

> 'Come, girls, beat your fists
> Down upon your breasts
> And shred your dresses.'

By analogy, 'Maidenhead, maidenhead, where have you gone?' a dialogue between a girl and Virginity personified, was also performed by a chorus (or at least by more than one singer).

Other songs seem to involve a solo singer and chorus of dancers. The following fragment is a good example:

> And this next charming ditty I –
> In honour of my girls –
> Shall sing out prettily.

It is implicit here that the singer is addressing an audience, i.e. this is a public performance for people other than the singer and her girls. The girls she so charmingly flatters, however, were probably present as well and dancing during the performance. 'Girls, chase the violet-bosomed Muses' bright' suggests a similar situation: the singer states explicitly that she is too old to dance and exhorts 'girls' to engage in the choral activities she used to enjoy. Again, the singer is presumably playing the lyre while a chorus danced.

But which of Sappho's poems were performed solo? This becomes a difficult question. One ancient source does mention Sappho's 'monodies' as separate from her nine books of lyric songs, and, as we have seen, the singer of 'Abanthis, please pick up your lyre' exhorts Abanthis to sing solo. However, not even the mention of Sappho by name as a speaker in a poem requires us to conclude that a chorus did not perform it. Since in some victory odes of Pindar and in the *parabaseis* of Aristophanes' comedies the chorus speaks on behalf of the poet in the first-person singular, a chorus may have performed even those poems of Sappho which give the impression one is overhearing 'personal' communication, such as an intimate conversation or monologue. Furthermore, any song in which a first-person plural ('we') appears is a candidate for choral performance, since this pronoun always refers to a group or a solo performer who wants to include others (an addressee, or a group, or all of humanity). Thus, we cannot be certain that even the most likely candidates – those in the first person – were performed solo. The Homericizing 'Idaos, then, the panting emissary' is a likely candidate for monodic performance with a lyre, and the singer would have performed it in the same manner as the bards in the *Odyssey* perform their songs. Odysseus himself provides the best description of bardic performance:

I say that nothing is more delightful than when mirth takes hold
of a whole people, and banqueters, seated in fitting order, listen
to a bard. Beside them tables stand full of bread and meat, and
a cup-bearer draws off wine from the mixing bowl and carries it
around and pours it into the cups. To my mind this seems the
most beautiful thing there is.

(Homer, *Odyssey* 9.5–11)

In most instances it is impossible to say whether the speaker
is a chorus or a soloist or even whether a given speaker is
Sappho. In discussions of performance context, as with most
things having to do with Sappho, we must content ourselves
with probabilities.

Woman, Poet and Woman Poet

It is difficult to talk about Sappho as a woman poet. One can
make statements like Strabo's (64 BCE–24 CE): 'in all of
recorded history I know of no woman who even came close to
rivalling her as a poet' (*Geography*, 13.2.3). With this kind of
classification, however, one runs the risk of relegating Sappho
to a separate 'female' league for poetry and overlooking
what she owes to her predecessors (Homer in particular), what
she has in common with her contemporaries (Alcaeus in par-
ticular) and how greatly she influences subsequent poetry. In
contrast to Strabo, Plutarch (46–120 CE) makes the useful
observation:

If, by comparing Sappho's poems with Anacreon's, we show . . .
that the art of poetry . . . is not different when practiced by men
and by women but the same, will anyone be able to find just
cause to reject our argument?

(*Virtues of Women* 243b)

The art is the same – Sappho fits squarely into the development
of poetry from Homeric epic to Greek lyric. She appropriates
themes, epithets and other diction from Homer, and in this she
is no different from male lyric poets such as Archilochus and

Alcaeus. In fact, the style of Sappho and Alcaeus is similar enough that scholars dispute whether certain fragments in the Lesbian dialect should be ascribed to one or the other of them. Furthermore, Sappho is greatly influential on subsequent poets, both female and male. Take this example: the Sapphic stanza, which she popularized and may have invented (some attribute it to Alcaeus), becomes a fixed form in Western literature. The Roman poets Catullus (84–54 BCE) and Horace (65–27 BCE) compose Sapphics in Latin and, in the modern period, Algernon Charles Swinburne (1837–1909), Allen Ginsberg (1926–97) and the contemporary American poet Tim Steele (b. 1948) in *Sapphics Against Anger* adapt the form to English prosody. The mainstream of Western poetry flows through Sappho and on down through the centuries. That she happens to be female, in this respect, is immaterial.

Sappho does have conventionally feminine interests. As we have seen, she exhibits a rich and intimate knowledge of toilette and fashion. She composes many songs for weddings, which were traditionally a female responsibility in Ancient Greek society. The question remains, however: was Sappho a feminist? In Ancient Greek literature male poets tend not simply to portray women as lecherous but to attribute to them a species of lust different from that of males: a subhuman and automatic reflex, an animalistic urge. Sappho is important because she gives a fully human voice to female desire for the first time in Western literature. Since she defiantly chooses the quintessential love-object Helen of Troy as her freethinking agent, she seems fully conscious of the revolutionary claim she is making.

NOTES

1. Gregory Nagy interprets the rock as a boundary marker between the worlds of the living and the dead ('Phaethon, Sappho's Phaon, and the White Rock of Leukas: "Reading" the Symbols of Greek Lyric', in Greene 1996, pp. 35–57).
2. Except where noted, I cite the texts of Sappho and Alcaeus from *Sappho et Alcaeus: Fragmenta*, ed. Eva-Maria Voigt (1971).

3. Holt Parker, 'Sappho Schoolmistress', *Transactions of the American Philological Association* 123 (1993), p. 314.
4. Burnett 1983, p. 210.
5. Martin West, 'A New Sappho Poem', *Times Literary Supplement*, no. 5334 (24 June 2005), p. 8.
6. Parker, 'Sappho Schoolmistress', pp. 339–51.
7. Burnett 1983, p. 209.
8. Wilson 1996, p. 104.
9. Burnett 1983, p. 297.
10. Calame 1996, p. 114.
11. Ibid., p. 121.
12. Chris Bennett, 'Concerning "Sappho Schoolmistress"', *Transactions of the American Philological Association* 124 (1994), p. 345.
13. Page 1955, p. 42.
14. Jack Winkler, 'Gardens of the Nymphs: Public and Private in Sappho's Lyrics', in Greene 1996, p. 108.
15. Walter Burkert, *Greek Religion* (1985), p. 155.
16. Sissa 1990, p. 98.
17. Wilson 1996, p. 145.
18. Page 1955, p. 27.
19. Skinner 2005, p. 59.
20. Winkler, 'Gardens of the Nymphs', p. 95.
21. *Hudson Review* 60:4 (Winter 2008), pp. 591–2.
22. Mary Lefkowitz, 'Critical Stereotypes and the Poetry of Sappho', in Greene 1996, p. 33.
23. Dubois 1995, p. 79.
24. Stigers 1977, p. 92.
25. Burnett 1983, p. 229.
26. Segal 1996, p. 59 (his emphasis).
27. Lardinois 1996, p. 159.

Further Reading

Burnett, Anne Pippin, *Three Archaic Poets: Archilochus, Alcaeus, Sappho* (1983). Comprehensive treatment of Sappho's poems with historical background and deep, thorough readings of all the major fragments.

Calame, Claude, 'Sappho's Group: An Initiation into Womanhood', in Greene 1996, pp. 113–24. This seminal essay argues that Sappho's group was a religious organization in which adolescent girls underwent a rite of passage into womanhood.

Dover, Kenneth J., *Greek Homosexuality* (1989). This landmark study of homosexuality in the Ancient Greek world focuses on the man–boy pattern of relationships in Athens.

Dowden, K., *Death and the Maiden: Girls' Initiation Rites in Greek Mythology* (1989). A fascinating but highly speculative book which uses myth to reconstruct rituals of initiation in prehistoric Bronze Age Greece.

Dubois, Page, *Sappho Is Burning* (1995). A collection of her essays which offers nuanced and sensitive readings of most of Sappho's fragments, along with critiques of Foucault and feminist theory. It is best suited to graduate students and advanced academics.

Greene, Ellen (ed.), *Reading Sappho: Contemporary Approaches* (1996). A collection of essays covering a range of themes, including Sappho's language and relationship with oral tradition, her social context and her eroticism.

Lardinois, André, 'Subject and Circumstance in Sappho's Poetry', *Transactions of the American Philological Association* 124 (1994), pp. 57–84. Refutes the theory that Sappho performed her poems solo at symposia for women of her own age and argues that, for many fragments, public choral performance is more likely.

—, 'Who Sang Sappho's Songs?', in Greene 1996, pp. 150–72. Argues that far more of the extant fragments of Sappho were originally performed by a chorus than had been traditionally maintained.

Page, Denys L., *An Introduction to the Study of Ancient Lesbian Poetry* (1955). This classic (but dated) treatment provides texts, translations and commentaries for the best-preserved fragments and fits most of the remaining fragments into useful essays on Sappho's style and character.

Segal, Charles, 'Eros and Incantation: Sappho and Oral Poetry', in Greene 1996, pp. 58–75. Argues that Sappho uses repetition, alliteration, assonance and other stylistic elements typical in Greek religious and magical song to produce an incantatory effect.

Sissa, Giulia, *Greek Virginity* tr. Arthur Goldhammer (1990). Studies images of matrons and virgins in the Ancient Greek world in order to determine how the female body was conceived.

Skinner, Marilyn, *Sexuality in Greek and Roman Culture* (2005). This authoritative reference work provides an inclusive and up-to-date history of sexuality in Greco-Roman culture, along with a bibliography for in-depth study of particular issues.

Stigers, Eva Stehle, 'Retreat from the Male: Catullus 62 and Sappho's Erotic Flowers', *Ramus* 6 (1977), pp. 83–103. As part of an interpretation of Catullus 62, Stigers argues that flowers are simultaneously associated with innocence and eroticism in the poems of Sappho.

Wilson, Lyn Heatherly, *Sappho's Sweet-Bitter Songs: Configurations of Female and Male in Ancient Greek Lyric* (1996). Though flawed by preconceived and anachronistic notions of masculinity and femininity, this study does provide sensitive readings of individual fragments.

A Note on the Text and Translation

It is important to point out that Sappho, as far as we know, did not gather her poems into a collection. Since society on the island of Lesbos was largely preliterate during her lifetime, she would have assumed that her poems would survive by being memorized rather than committed to papyrus. We owe those scraps of Sappho that have come down to us to two Alexandrian scholars, Aristophanes of Byzantium (c. 257–180 BCE) and Aristarchus of Samothrace (c. 220–c. 143 BCE): they arranged the poems which survived to the third and second centuries BCE into nine books. Each poem was selected for inclusion in the first eight books on the basis of its metre. The first book, for example, contained roughly 1,300 verses and included poems composed in the Sapphic stanza. Two epithalamia in this metre ('Because once on a time you were' and 'And may the maidens all night long') appeared at the end. Along the same lines the wedding poem 'Idaos, then, the panting emissary' appeared last in the second book, which consisted of poems in a metre readily accommodating Homeric diction. Books 3–8 consisted of poems in a variety of other metres, sometimes with two or more metres per book. The ninth and final book, called 'The Epithalamia', consisted of those wedding poems which did not did not fit into any of the eight groupings. Though Books 2–9 were probably shorter than the first, the complete collection may well have included around 9,000 lines.

Tullius Laurea, the learned freedman and librarian for Cicero (106–43 BCE), attests in an epigram that the nine-book collection survived into the first century BCE (*Anthologia Palatina* 7.17), and Sappho's poetry was influential on the Roman poets

Catullus and Horace. Subsequently the depredations of time, chance and puritanical taste so reduced the number of poems available that the Byzantine grammarian John Tzetzes of Constantinople (1110–80 CE) could declare 'time has frittered away Sappho and her works, her lyre and songs' (*On the Meters of Pindar* 20–22). Frustrated as he was, Tzetzes still seems to have had access to more of Sappho than we do. But those texts were probably destroyed when the Fourth Crusade sacked and burned Constantinople in 1204, and for almost seven centuries the world knew only those poems of Sappho which happened to have been preserved as citations in the works of other authors.

In the 1870s excavation at the oasis of Fayum in the Nile valley uncovered a number of eighth-century-CE manuscripts, and several fragments of Sappho were among them. Subsequent excavations among the nearby refuse heaps of Oxyrhynchus (a Greco-Egyptian provincial capital) turned up a vast quantity of papyrus fragments ranging in date from the first to the tenth centuries CE. Much of this had served as cartonnage which filled the empty space in coffins or had been wadded up to stuff the insides of mummies. One fragment of Sappho, in fact, was recovered from a mummified crocodile.

Even with the Oxyrhynchus fragments, we had until recently only one complete poem, 'Subtly bedizened Aphrodite', cited in Dionysius of Halicarnassus' *On Style*. In 2004, however, scholars at the University of Cologne determined that a previously unascribed papyrus contained portions of three of Sappho's poems. One of these provided the missing half of a fragment that had been published in 1922, and the Greek text of a new, nearly complete poem was presented to the world by Martin West, along with a brief introduction and an English translation, in *The Times Literary Supplement* (no. 5334, 24 June 2005, p. 8). I am optimistic that future papyrus finds and advances in laser-scanning technology will recover even more of the thousands of lines of Sappho that have, perhaps for millennia, been unknown to the world.

In addition to these two poems, I have translated those fragments or parts of fragments that are best able to stand on their own in English. Containing 78 of the roughly 230 fragments, this edition omits most of those that consist only of a word or phrase and all of those that are so tattered as to be indecipherable. I relied almost entirely on the text of Eva-Maria Voigt[1] and note those few instances in which I preferred the text of Lobel–Page[2] in the Index of First Lines. For 'Girls, chase the violet-bosomed Muses' bright' I have used West's Greek text. Translations from Classical authors other than Sappho are also my own. Punctuation and capitalization are editorial, and ellipses are used to indicate a lacuna in the source-text. I confess that, though Sappho's remains are usually fragments that are themselves fragmentary, I have done my best to create a sense of completeness and, on occasion, translated supplements proposed by scholars.

In preparation for this project I surveyed dozens of English translations and was disappointed to discover that contemporary editions neglected the formal elements of Sappho's poems and focused almost exclusively on their content. Since form and content are inseparable, the translator must find not only appropriate words for the original words but an appropriate form for the original form. Sappho did not compose free verse, and free-verse translations, however faithful they may be to her words, betray her poems by their very nature. Translations into the original metres are always interesting but are flawed in their methodology: the Sapphic stanza, for example, belongs to a quantitative (or length-based) metrical system and is not accurately represented by the same metrical scheme in our English qualitative (or stressed-based) system. Furthermore, the Aeolic Greeks grew up hearing the Sapphic stanza and similar rhythms and had associations with them, but, for English speakers, they do not have the same resonance. One wants to translate into a form which helps the reader feel the meaning of a poem. As Sapphic stanzas are still a novelty in English poetry, they would not be helpful to most readers. Since all of Sappho's poems are song-lyrics, I opted to translate them as English lyric poems. Rhyme, an important part of this tradition, is useful in translating Sappho for two reasons: (1) it is one of the ways English writers indicate that something is song-like; and (2) individual

lines within Sappho's poems had emphatic endings, usually two
long syllables, and rhyme preserves the integrity of the line
within the stanza in much the same way.

I wanted my translations to be real poems in their own right
which, when read aloud, would replicate the aural pleasure of
their originals. Scholars have argued that Sappho's language is
a form of enchantment, and I have tried to weave a similar rich
and bewitching texture of sound. To preserve the effect of the
Sapphic stanza I have most often used three lines of iambic
tetrameter followed by a dimetre. For the Homericizing frag-
ments I have employed the heroic couplet which Dryden's and
Pope's translations of Classical epic recommended to me. For
the brief fragments I chose metres and rhyme schemes which
would set a proper tone and give due weight to every precious
word. Departing from the numerical order of the scholarly
editions, I have gathered the poems and fragments under
general headings by subject and/or type. This arrangement
facilitates comparison and, I feel, results in a richer reading
experience. Out of a desire to prevent notes from cluttering the
translations or gathering in a heap at the back of the book, I
decided to present essential information in commentaries facing
each poem, fragment or group of fragments.

Sappho continues to amaze readers because she retained the
intensity of passion which we associate with the young even
into old age. She never grew out of desire, and we can greatly
admire her ardour.

NOTES

1. Eva-Maria Voigt (ed.), *Sappho et Alcaeus: Fragmenta* (1971).
2. Edgar Lobel and Denys Page (eds.), *Poetarum Lesbiorum Frag-
   menta* (1955).

Poems and Fragments

GODDESSES

This fragment survives on a potsherd (a fragment of broken pottery) inscribed by an unknown hand in the second century BCE. Our text begins with what was probably the second stanza of the original, and Aphrodite, in accordance with convention, would have been invoked in the first. The worshipper, who is not named, calls for divine aid in eucharistic terms. Though ostensibly a kletic hymn (or hymn to summon a deity: see Introduction, p. xxvi), the poem uses colloquial rather than formal language.

Whereas other kletic hymns summon the deity from habitual haunts, this portion of the poem creates the place that will receive its heavenly visitor. The lush, vivid description of the sanctuary has provoked various interpretations: some scholars argue that Sappho describes a real shrine in a precise cultic environment; others, that the sacred precinct is a metaphor for women's sexuality. The landscape is distinctly Aphrodisiac: Burnett calls the fragment a 'portrait in which the goddess's best-known attributes and parts are rendered as bits of landscape ... Gardens, apples, perfumes, roses, field-flowers and horses all serve to remind Aphrodite of herself, as she is worshipped in her various cults' (1983, p. 263).

The apple orchards are *charien* ('charming') – a word most often used of personal charm. Apples, the most important fruit in Sappho, symbolize virginity in other songs. She gives us the earliest appearance of *libanōtos* ('frankincense') in Greek literature. The thick roses, which belong to the spring, and the apples, which belong to the autumn, suggest the perennial growing season of the Golden Age. In addition, the floral imagery evokes the blossoming fields where, at least in literature, erotic encounters often take place. Here substance shades into insubstantiality: the roses turn to shadows and the leaves 'drip slumber'. All of the landscape elements induce not just normal sleep but *kōma*, a special sleep brought on by supernatural means.

In the final stanza Aphrodite pours out nectar or wine mixed with nectar for the celebrants – a liquid representing the divine presence among them. This mixture, like Aphrodite's arrival, integrates the mortal and immortal.

Leave Crete and sweep to this blest temple
Where apple-orchard's elegance
Is yours, and smouldering altars, ample
Frankincense.

Here under boughs a bracing spring
Percolates, roses without number
Umber the earth and, rustling,
The leaves drip slumber.

Here budding flowers possess a sunny
Pasture where steeds could graze their fill,
And the breeze feels as gentle as honey . . .

Kypris, here in the present blend
Your nectar with pure festal glee.
Fill gilded bowls and pass them round
Lavishly.

In these fragments Aphrodite Pandemos ('of all the people') influences, for better or worse, the daily lives of individuals. 'Sweet mother, I can't take shuttle in hand' is a song based on popular tradition, a refined version of a work-song such as girls sang over the loom while weaving. The shuttle is a tool used for plying the horizontal weft threads through the vertical warp threads on a loom. Throughout Greek and Roman literature weaving is the activity of a female head-of-household in an ideal home. Helen of Troy weaves in an attempt to legitimize her adulterous affair with Paris (*Iliad* 3.125–9). Penelope weaves a death shroud for her father-in-law Laertes both as a delaying tactic and as confirmation of her loyalty to her husband Odysseus (*Odyssey* 2.96–102). When the goddess Kalypso tries to replicate a 'mortal' domestic home life for Odysseus, she also weaves (*Odyssey* 5.61–2).

The tone rapidly fluctuates between torment and tenderness, and a mere four lines convey the girl's coming of age: the mother and loom on one side, the boy and Aphrodite on the other are playing tug of war, and the girl is torn between them. There are two possible futures for the girl who speaks these lines: she may go on to marry and become a female head-of-household like her mother (and keep on weaving), or, under the influence of Aphrodite, she may give in to her sexual attraction to the boy and be ruined like the flower in 'A hillside hyacinth shepherds treaded flat'. Desire here is simultaneously violent and tender, and we find a similar bitter-sweetness in 'That impossible predator'.

Though 'luck-bringing' Hermes is the deity associated with success in games of chance, Sappho invokes Aphrodite in 'Since I have cast my lot, please, golden-crowned', thereby suggesting that matters of the heart are comparable to gambling. Aphrodite Kypria (of Cyprus) also wears a golden crown in the fifth and sixth Homeric Hymns, and we are told there that she 'rules over the walled cities of all sea-surrounded Cyprus' (6.2).

Sweet mother, I can't take shuttle in hand.
There is a boy, and lust
Has crushed my spirit – just
As gentle Aphrodite planned.

Since I have cast my lot, please, golden-crowned
Aphrodite, let me win this round!

This song breaks down into the tripartite structure of a kletic hymn (see Introduction, p. xxvi). Whereas the singer conventionally commemorates a mythic event, Sappho here cites one of a series of past personal visits from Aphrodite.

In the opening stanza Sappho addresses the goddess and asks for relief in formulaic terms. Aphrodite flies down from Olympus in a chariot drawn by sparrows, which were associated with lasciviousness and fecundity, and their flesh and eggs eaten as aphrodisiacs. Though there are several references to sparrows as a means of conveyance in subsequent Greek literature, swans become the traditional yoke animals of Aphrodite (Venus) in the Roman poets.

The formal tone then gives way to the familiar. Aphrodite's smile is particularly striking. Homer characterizes Aphrodite with the epithet *philommeidēs* (smile-loving), a softened form of the title *philommedēs* (genital-loving). The focus on her smile here may also be meant to evoke the 'Archaic Smile' found on statuary during the Archaic period. In Greek literature gods not infrequently interact with their favourite mortals but Aphrodite exhibits an exceptional familiarity with Sappho – the closest parallel is Athena's banter with Odysseus in *Odyssey* 13.

Most scholars assume that Aphrodite promises to compel the girl to reciprocate Sappho's ardour. Anne Carson points out that Aphrodite says only that the girl will 'pursue, give gifts and love' – Sappho is not specified as the object. Aphrodite may promise only that 'in the course of time the beloved will naturally and inevitably become a lover, and will almost inevitably suffer rejection at least once' ('The Justice of Aphrodite in Sappho Fr. 1', in Greene 1996, pp. 227–8.)

In the final stanza Sappho rounds out her allusions to Homeric epic by asking Aphrodite to be her *summachos* ('ally in battle'). She thus substitutes her trials in love for those of a hero in battle and elevates matters of the heart to the same level as war.

Subtly bedizened Aphrodite,
Deathless daughter of Zeus, Wile-weaver,
I beg you, Empress, do not smite me
With anguish and fever

But come as often, on request,
(Hearing me, heeding from afar,)
You left your father's gleaming feast,
Yoked team to car,

And came. Fair sparrows in compact
Flurries of winged rapidity
Cleft sky and over a gloomy tract
Brought you to me –

And there they were, and you, sublime
And smiling with immortal mirth,
Asked what was wrong? why I, this time,
Called you to earth?

What was my mad heart dreaming of? –
'Who, Sappho, at a word, must grow
Again receptive to your love?
Who wronged you so?

'She who shuns love soon will pursue it,
She who scorns gifts will send them still:
That girl will learn love, though she do it
Against her will.'

Come to me now. Drive off this brutal
Distress. Accomplish what my pride
Demands. Come, please, and in this battle
Stand at my side.

The story of Aphrodite's love for the doomed Adonis is another example of Sappho's interest in myths which involve erotic female empowerment; others include Dawn and Tithonous, and Artemis' request for eternal virginity. In his cult, Adonis is an annually renewed, ever-youthful vegetation god, a life–death–rebirth deity whose transformations are tied to the calendar. We hear of two fathers for him, both of whom are eponyms which suggest possible places of origin: Hesiod names Phoenix (for Phoenicia) and Classical sources name Kyprus (for Cyprus). Walter Burkert questions whether Adonis had not from the very beginning come to Greece from the East with Aphrodite (*Greek Religion* (1985), p. 177). Though this fragment is our earliest evidence for the Adonis cult, annual ritual lamentation for his death and burial in a lettuce bed (which we find in other brief fragments of Sappho) accord well with accounts in subsequent sources. We are told that at the Athenian Adonia women gathered on rooftops and engaged in loud obscenity (Aristophanes, *Lysistrata* 387–96), and celebrants prepared gardens of fennel and lettuce (regarded as an anaphrodisiac). These plants spring up and wither quickly, and the women may have been lamenting impotence as well as the untimely death of the vegetation god. Beating one's breast and rending one's garments were part of ritual lamentation, itself a part of funerary rites in general. Mourners would also cut their hair short and lacerate their cheeks. The ritual context here suggests that the Sapphic community, at least on occasion, served a religious function.

'A full moon shone' was probably the beginning of a poem that described nocturnal worship. One would love to know which deity the devotees are worshipping: the lunar goddesses Artemis and Hecate? Aphrodite? Lunar imagery is prominent in a number of other songs (see, e.g., 'Moon and the Pleiades go down' and 'Star clusters near the fair moon dim').

'Kytherea, precious
Adonis is nearly dead.
How should we proceed?'

'Come, girls, beat your fists
Down upon your breasts
And shred your dresses.'

A full moon shone,
And around the shrine
Stood devotees
Poised and in place.

Sappho almost exclusively invokes female deities. Here we meet the
Graces (or *Kharites*, related to our 'Charity') who often attend on
Aphrodite in art and literature. They were goddesses of grace, mirth,
floral adornment and relaxation – in short, the pleasures of life. The
Graces have the character of unsuspicious maidens and, in some
sources, names and specific prerogatives:

> And the daughter of Okeanos, Eurynome,
> who had a much-praised figure, bore [Zeus]
> three radiant-cheeked Graces: Aglaia (Splendour),
> Euphrosyne (Merriment) and lovely Thalia (Festivity),
> from all of whose glancing eyes limb-loosening love streamed,
> And their gaze shines beautifully from beneath their brows.
>   (Hesiod, *Theogony* 907–11)

The god Eros himself is described as the 'Limb-Loosener' in 'That
impossible predator', and 'limb-loosening love' is central to several of
Sappho's erotic songs. She applies the epithet (or characteristic title)
'rosy-forearmed' to Dawn (Eos) in 'Girls, chase the violet-bosomed
Muses' bright'.

'Now, Dika, weave the aniseed together, flower and stem' is one of
the fragments in which Sappho gives the impression that the listener
is overhearing a private conversation. Dika, probably a pet name from
'Mnasidika', contributes to the intimate setting. In a brief fragment
we learn that 'Mnasidika is more shapely than plush Gyrinno' (82a
Voigt). Anise or aniseed (*Pimpinella anisum*) is a sweet-smelling,
liquorice-flavoured flowering plant, still used to make Turkish raki,
Greek ouzo and for a variety of other purposes. Athenaeus cites this
fragment as evidence that 'the more a thing is bedecked with flowers,
the more delightful it is to the gods' (*Scholars at Dinner* 15.674e). It
is uncertain whether it was performed as solo or choral song but
chorus members did wear floral adornments similar to those described
here.

> Untainted Graces
> With wrists like roses,
> Please come close,
> You daughters of Zeus.

Now, Dika, weave the aniseed together, flower and
    stem,
With your soft hands, crown yourself with a lovely
    diadem
Because the blessèd Graces grant gifts to the garlanded
And snub the worshipper with no flowers on her head.

'Come close, you precious' is probably the beginning of a kletic hymn to the Muses and the Graces. Daughters of Zeus and Mnemosyne (Memory), the Muses are goddesses of music, song and dance, and a source of inspiration to poets. In ancient Greek vase painting the Muses are often depicted as young women with a variety of musical instruments including flutes and lyres. Their number is eventually fixed at nine, and they acquire names and specific spheres of influence – Calliope, the muse of epic poetry; Erato, muse of erotic poetry, etc. On Mt Olympus they sing festive songs in the dining hall of the immortals. On earth the Muses inspire a poet to speak truthfully about subjects in which he or she has no personal expertise. After warning the poet Hesiod that 'they know how to tell many lies that sound like truth' but also 'know how to sing reality, when [they] wish', they proceed to fill him with the ability to sing of the past and the future (*Theogony* 26–8). On the Graces, see p. 12.

Maximus of Tyre (125–185 CE) claims that Sappho is delivering 'Here is the reason: it is wrong' to her daughter on her deathbed. Though it is not certain that Sappho had a daughter and one can only wonder how she would have had time and energy to versify this before expiring, Maximus may well have had access to more details from a more complete version of the song. On the Musicians' House, see pp. xx–xxi.

Come close, you precious
Graces and Muses
With beautiful tresses.

Here is the reason: it is wrong
To play a funeral song
In the Musicians' House –
It simply would not be decorous.

Sappho often mentions and even addresses lyres. After her death she was associated, like the Muses, with the lyre, and subsequent art and literature frequently portray her as a Muse. Catullus 35.16–17 refers to a 'Sapphic Muse', and we find the following assertion (attributed to Plato) in the *Palatine Anthology* 9.506: 'some say there are nine Muses: how cheap! Look – Sappho of Lesbos is the tenth'. Sappho is credited with the invention of the *pēctis* (large many-stringed lyre) and the *plectrum* (pick for a lyre), and Plutarch, *On Music* 16.1136c, claims that she invented the Mixolydian mode (an emotional mode, suited to tragedy).

In 'God-crafted product of the tortoise-shell' Sappho personifies her lyre. Hermogenes, *Kinds of Style* 2.4, preserves this fragment as an example of the 'sweet effect' which 'the ascription of conscious choice to things incapable of it produces'. 'He is unrivalled, like a Lesbian' became a proverbial expression for excellence in song.

In *Anthology* 3.4.12 Stobaeus informs us that Sappho addressed 'But when you lie dead' to an uneducated woman; Plutarch in different places claims it is addressed to 'a wealthy woman' and 'an uncultivated and ignorant woman'. Except in a few special cases, Hades' hall is not a place of punishment like the Christian Hell: it is a gloomy detention area where the *psychai* (or 'breaths') of the deceased remain forever as an insubstantial images or 'shades' of themselves. It is not at all painful but very dull. We find in this fragment the same concern for immortality which we find in 'I declare'. The region Pieria takes its name from Mt Pierus in ancient Thrace (now north-eastern mainland Greece). The Muses were held to dwell on this mountain and a local spring was regarded as a source of wisdom and inspiration. 'The Pierian spring' becomes a symbol for poetic wisdom in general, as in Alexander Pope's *Essay on Criticism* (1711):

> A little learning is a dangerous thing;
> Drink deep, or taste not the Pierian spring:
> There shallow draughts intoxicate the brain,
> And drinking largely sobers us again.
>
> (215–18)

God-crafted product of the tortoise shell,
Come to me; Lyre, be voluble.

He is unrivalled, like a Lesbian
Musician matched with other men.

But when you lie dead
No one will notice later or feel sad
Because you gathered no sprays from the roses
Of the Pierian Muses.

Once lost in Hades' hall
You will be homeless and invisible –
Another shadow flittering back and forth
With shadows of no worth.

DESIRE AND
DEATH-LONGING

Eros is the god of ardent desire. He appears either as a universal principle promoting procreation or the mischievous son of Aphrodite, armed with bow and arrows. In Hesiod's *Theogony* Eros is 'limb-loosening', and in Homer a hero's limbs are loosened in battle when he loses consciousness or dies. Sappho combines these traditions as Eros here loosens limbs by dismembering a body. Though it is difficult to determine exactly what rough beast the god Eros is supposed to be, his predation is both pleasant and painful, and this bitter-sweetness characterizes Sappho's erotic songs.

'Like a gale smiting an oak' is in essence an epic simile like those which regularly appear in Homer's *Iliad* and *Odyssey*. By using this literary device Sappho again suggests that matters of the heart are comparable to military matters.

'But a strange longing to pass on' is one of a number of erotic songs which express death-longing. Acheron is a lake in the underworld across which the boatman Charon ferries the shades (or ghosts) of the dead. Lotuses (probably the *Ziziphus lotus*), associated with forgetful-ness, grow along its shore. Sappho handles the underworld motif in a conventional manner, and Giuliana Lanata observes that 'the relative fixity of its formulation expresses a moment typical of the Sapphic experience of Eros, destined to repeat itself more times in analogous situations' ('Sappho's Amatory Language', in Greene 1996, p. 19).

The name 'Gongyla' appears in the patchy lines which precede our fragment, and we are informed elsewhere that she was a student of Sappho from abroad. The lost lines may have contained a conversation between Sappho (or at least an 'I') and another person, who scholars suggest is 'Hermas' (or Hermes) on the basis of the '–as' that appears in the damaged text. This possibility is appealing because we also have divine epiphanies in other poems which, it would seem, have a similar structure. Hermes Psychopompus (or 'conductor of souls' to the under-world) would then be the addressee of the speech.

That impossible predator,
Eros the Limb-Loosener,
Bitter-sweetly and afresh
Savages my flesh.

Like a gale smiting an oak
On mountainous terrain,
Eros, with a stroke,
Shattered my brain.

But a strange longing to pass on
Seizes me, and I need to see
Lotuses on the dewy banks of Acheron.

Longinus (fl. first century CE) has preserved this famous fragment in his literary treatise *On the Sublime*. The dramatic setting is simple: the female narrator sees a beloved girl talking and laughing with a man and then proceeds to describe her reaction to the sight. Though the scenario is anachronistic, I have found it helpful to imagine her in the doctor's office listing the symptoms of her love disease, many of which are paralleled in Homer but not as symptoms of love. Archilochus of Paros (680–c. 645 BCE) also describes the love disease in Homeric terms:

> Just this sort of lust for love crouched at my heart
> And, after he had stolen the gentle senses from my breast,
> Kept pouring thick mist down over my eyes.
> > (Martin West, *Iambi et Elegi Graeci*,
> > Vol. I (1971), fr. 191)

We find the only occurrence of *kardia* ('heart') and *glōssa* ('tongue') in Sappho here as part of a similarly physical description. Since our word 'heart' carries sentimental baggage inappropriate to the Greek *kardia*, I opted for the medical 'ventricles'. Thin fire and thunder in the ears are not found as symptoms of love before this poem.

Scholarship tends to focus on the question: why is the speaker so agitated? Is it jealousy because a man is enjoying the company of her beloved? Or a sympathetic reaction resulting from the speaker's vicarious experience of what the man is experiencing? If there were a love triangle we would expect to hear more about the speaker's rival. He remains indefinite – we hear nothing about him after the first stanza. He serves only a formal function and is godlike only because he sits 'face to face' with the girl. However, we hear no more of the girl after the first stanza either. Instead of an objectification of the beloved we are given an objectification of the lover: she is broken down piece by piece.

Catullus wrote an adaptation of this song in the original Sapphic metre, and the following stanza is usually appended:

> Idleness, Catullus, is destroying you;
> Idleness is what delights you and stirs you to passion;
> Idleness before now has proved the ruin of kings
> And prosperous cities.
> > (51.13–16)

That fellow strikes me as god's double,
Couched with you face to face, delighting
In your warm manner, your amiable
Talk and inviting

Laughter – the revelation flutters
My ventricles, my sternum and stomach.
The least glimpse, and my lost voice stutters,
Refuses to come back

Because my tongue is shattered. Gauzy
Flame runs radiating under
My skin; all that I see is hazy,
My ears all thunder.

Sweat comes quickly, and a shiver
Vibrates my frame. I am more sallow
Than grass and suffer such a fever
As death should follow.

But I must suffer further, worthless
As I am . . .

This fragment is one of several in which Sappho recounts a past conversation framed by a poetic present (see 'Subtly bedizened Aphrodite'). Here the conversation is about activities even further in the past. It is unclear whether Sappho the poet, Sappho the character (who is named) or her female addressee speaks the first line, and it is difficult to determine whether the sentence is merely a hyperbolic commonplace (like 'I almost died from embarrassment') or heartfelt expression.

Myrrh is the reddish-brown dried resin of the tree *Commiphora myrrha*, native to north-eastern Africa. Mixed in oil, myrrh has been used for embalming and for anointment in the Eastern Orthodox Church. It is still used in perfumes and lotions.

In Sappho we often find erotic emotion and experience expressed in stylized and ritualized ways. These patterns serve to convert the private and specific into the universal and the generic. The 'good times' of which Sappho reminds the girl primarily involve flowers and garlands – the sorts of adornments which choral performers would wear (compare 'Now, Dika, weave the aniseed together, flower and stem'). Here, as in 'Off in Sardis', thoughts of flowers bind females together once they have been separated. The list of activities becomes increasingly intimate: we progress from weaving garlands and necklaces to perfuming the girl's hair and eventually to the satisfaction of desire on a bed. It is remarkable that even sexual release becomes part of the ritualized pattern. Lyn Wilson observes 'the song seems designed to give comfort in a way which would be almost maternal if it did not linger over erotic details' (1996, p. 127). The first-person plural pronoun may expand in this song to refer to all the members of the group. This pronoun and the description of floral adornments make it a likely candidate for choral performance.

'In all honesty, I want to die.'

Leaving for good after a good long cry,
She said: 'We both have suffered terribly,
But, Sappho, it is hard to say goodbye.'

I said: 'Go with my blessing if you go
Always remembering what we did. To me
You have meant everything, as you well know.

'Yet, lest it slip your mind, I shall review
Everything we have shared – the good times, too:

'You culled violets and roses, bloom and stem,
Often in spring and I looked on as you
Wove a bouquet into a diadem.

'Time and again we plucked lush flowers, wed
Spray after spray in strands and fastened them
Around your soft neck; you perfumed your head

'Of glossy curls with myrrh – lavish infusions
In queenly quantities – then on a bed
Prepared with fleecy sheets and yielding cushions,

'Sated your craving . . .'

The first two fragments provide contrasting statements of anger and conciliation. 'May gales and anguish sweep elsewhere' is a curse. It is striking that the speaker calls both external (gales) and internal (anguish) afflictions down upon an enemy. In 'But I am hardly some backbiter bent' the narrator protests so much about her lack of malignance that the effect is an ironic awareness that she probably is all that she denies.

The next two provide contrasting descriptions of hot and cold. Julian the Apostate (331–363 CE), the last polytheistic Roman emperor, preserved 'You were at hand' in a literary epistle addressed to the deceased Iamblicus (245–325 CE), a Syrian Neoplatonist philosopher who defended polytheistic cult practice. Julian adds: 'Indeed you did come; because of your letter you came even though you were absent.' The fragment is exquisitely beautiful but difficult to translate because a lover who is driven crazy by a burning desire is now too much of a cliché even for pop songs. In 'Cold grew' we are told that pigeons are folding their wings to warm themselves. I have translated the feminine definite article as 'ladies' on the assumption that this image was originally a metaphor for human behaviour.

May gales and anguish sweep elsewhere
The killer of my character.

But I am hardly some backbiter bent
On vengeance; no, my heart is lenient.

You were at hand,
And I broke down raving –
My craving a fire
That singed my mind,
A brand you quenched.

Cold grew
The spirits of the ladies;
They drew
Their wings close to their bodies.

The Sapphic persona thrives on activity and passion. Deprived of these things, she lapses into a languorous state. Lunar imagery is common in the poems of Sappho (compare 'Off in Sardis' and 'Star clusters near the fair moon dim'), and the moon is consistently associated with feminine beauty. In 'Moon and the Pleiades go down' it vanishes from the narrator's view. The Pleiades (or Seven Sisters) is a prominent star cluster in the constellation Taurus, and in mythology seven nymphs who attend the goddess Artemis.

'Peace, you never seemed so tedious' is difficult to interpret and to translate. *Irēna*, the addressee, is either the abstraction Peace or a proper name. I have opted for the apostrophe to Peace, and the fragment thus expresses a general ennui or frustration probably in anticipation of someone's arrival. But, if addressed to an Irena, it preserves an irritated remark to an annoying woman. This fragment exemplifies the difficulty of translating scraps that have come down to us without context: the tone and meaning of the couplet here hangs on a word which has one of two radically different but equally possible meanings.

In 'Over eyelids dark night fell' the night is invisible because a person's eyes have already closed. This fragment may, in fact, be the source for Catullus' expansion on Sappho's 'all that I see is hazy' in his adaptation of 'That fellow strikes me as god's double'. In Catullus' version (51) the speaker's 'eyes are covered by a twin night'.

Moon and the Pleiades go down.
Midnight and tryst pass by.
I, though, lie
Alone.

Peace, you never seemed so tedious
As now – no, never quite like this.

Over eyelids dark night fell
Invisible.

HER GIRLS AND FAMILY

We know that 'But I love extravagance' are the last two lines of a four-line epigram. Before the identification of an Oxyrhynchus fragment in 2003, it was assumed that this couplet was the conclusion of a longer poem that contained 'Girls, chase the violet-bosomed Muses' bright', and previous scholarship had interpreted it as such. On Athenaeus' introduction to these lines, see p. xxxiv.

'I truly do believe no maiden that will live' may simply mean: 'I think no girl will ever be as *sophos* (clever) as this one.' However, 'To look upon the sun' (a stock epic and tragic phrase meaning simply 'to live') raises the register, and the lines may express admiration for a girl who has already come to appreciate all that the sun symbolizes in the preceding poem. The sun here contains, in the abstract, qualities of shiny luxury items – glitter and glamour.

'Stand and face me, dear; release' exemplifies the importance of eye contact, especially between lovers and rivals, in Greek literature. As we have seen, Sappho reveals an intimate, almost medical knowledge of the symptoms of love in 'That fellow strikes me as god's double'. Dilated pupils signal a state of arousal and are thus more attractive. In addition, the ancients assumed that light reflected from the eyes was emitted from the eyes themselves. For example, when Plato argues that the soul is the source of vision, he cites light rays coming from the eyes as evidence.

But I love extravagance,
And wanting it has handed down
The glitter and glamour of the sun
As my inheritance.

I truly do believe no maiden that will live
To look upon the brilliance of the sun
Ever will be contemplative
Like this one.

Stand and face me, dear; release
That fineness in your irises.

'May you bed down' may have been part of an epithalamium (or wedding poem). Theocritus (third century BCE) alludes to this fragment in *Epithalamium of Helen*, 49–58, during the final valediction and *makarismos* (blessing) of the couple:

> Farewell, bride, and, farewell, groom – you are the son of a mighty father.
> May Leto, Child-Rearing Leto, grant you fecundity;
> And Kypris, divine Kypris, to love one another in equal amount,
> and Zeus, the son of Kronos, Zeus, an imperishable prosperity
> Which will pass in turn from noble stock to noble scion.
> Sleep on, breathing affection and desire on one another's breast
> But do not forget to rise at dawn. For we shall come at dawn,
> As soon as the earliest riser, the rooster, raises his ruffled neck to crow.
> *Hymn, O Hymenaios, may you take joy in this marriage.*

'May you bed down' may have belonged to a similar context, and one of Sappho's very brief *makarismoi* fragments may have appeared shortly before it, such as fragment 117: 'Farewell, bride, and farewell, groom'.

The cryptic and haunting 'As for you girls, the gorgeous ones' is addressed to *paides* (girls) who are *kalai* (beautiful/gorgeous). The *kalai* may have been tantamount to an official title in Sappho's group. It is unclear what the speaker has in mind for them.

In 'What farm girl, garbed in fashions from the farm' the girl is criticized for not knowing how to present herself in an enticing manner. Athenaeus informs us that she is Sappho's rival Andromeda (*Scholars at Dinner* 1.21c). Though several other fragments linger over details of fashion, this one is interesting for its focus on the ankle area, which is an erogenous zone in Ancient Greek poetry. In 'Idaos, then, the panting emissary' Sappho refers to 'maids / With slim-tapering ankles'. As discussed in the Introduction, this fragment implies membership in an exclusive group, and at least one of the criteria for inclusion is knowledge of ways to dress attractively.

May you bed down,
Head to breast, upon
The flesh
Of a plush
Companion.

As for you girls, the gorgeous ones,
There will be no change in my plans.

What farm girl, garbed in fashions from the
     farm
And witless of the way
A hiked hem would display
Her ankles, captivates you with her charm?

In 'Off in Sardis' we first meet Atthis, who will also appear as the speaker's current beloved, a traitor who 'goes over' to the rival Andromeda, and an old flame. As in 'That fellow strikes me as god's double' and 'Abanthis, please pick your lyre', there is a triangular arrangement of characters: the speaker talks to Atthis about a girl who once admired Atthis greatly but has gone off to start a new life.

It is clear that the absent girl now resides in Sardis, the capital of Lydia, and often has Atthis in mind. In the second complete stanza Sappho appropriates 'rosy-fingered', a famous Homeric epithet of the goddess Dawn, for an elaborate lunar simile. Red moons are a visually striking phenomenon which occur when a concentration of particles in the air (i.e. dust or smoke) scatter the short and intermediate wavelengths of light (violet, blue and yellow) and only the longer ones (orange and red) reach our eyes. Here the moon brings the dew and opens flowers. In addition to roses, we find chervil (*Anthriscus cerefolium*), an annual herb with white flowers related to parsley, and sweet clover or melilot (*Melilotus*), a plant which has flowers in a variety of colours.

Though the transition into the lunar simile is smooth, it is not clear where it ends and the poem returns to the literal world. One is left to ponder: what do the dew and the flowers have to do with Atthis and/or the girl who has gone away? The images seem both to belong to the 'flower-rich fallows' on which the moon shines in the third stanza and to be what the departed girl in the fifth stanza encounters when she wanders off alone. The girl walks under the very moon to which she was compared. The poem moves without any explicit indication from a figurative night to a real one, from the world of the simile to the 'real world' where the girl resides.

A tattered subsequent stanza (not translated) suggests that the distance between the three of them is bridged. It begins with 'to go there' and ends with the 'the middle'.

        . . . off in Sardis
And often turns her thoughts back to our shores.

The girl adored you more than anything,
As if you were a goddess –
But most of all she loved to hear you sing.

Now she outshines those dames with Lydian faces
Just as, when the sun
Has set, the rosy-fingered Moon surpasses

The stars surrounding her. With equal grace
She casts her lustre on
The flower-rich fallows and the sterile seas.

Dew is poured out in handsome fashion; lissome
Chervil unfurls; Rose
And Sweet Clover with heady flowers blossom.

Often on long walks she commemorates
How tender Atthis was.
Her fortune eats at her inconstant thoughts . . .

Sappho repeatedly removes memories from their specific contexts, generalizes and idealizes them, and then presents them in song as a form of consolation. 'You will have memories' preserves a part of this process. However, we are left to wonder just what beautiful things the speaker and addressee 'did back then' when they were young, which, the speaker asserts, will remain with the addressee throughout her life.

In 'I loved you once, years ago, Atthis' the speaker reveals her former affection for an Atthis, who was still a maiden and still in an awkward stage of adolescence. Through refinement she has acquired *charis* ('grace') but, by implication, lost many things, including an appealing innocence. In a Latin note the grammarian Terentianus Maurus (end of the second century CE) preserves the phrase that I have translated as the second line. I take his *sua* ('her own') as referring to Atthis' flower of virginity rather than the speaker's.

In the next fragment Atthis has turned the tables on the speaker and gone over to Andromeda, the rival in 'What farm girl, garbed in fashions from the farm'.

You will have memories
Because of what we did back then
When we were new at this,

Yes, we did many things, then – all
Beautiful . . .

I loved you once, years ago, Atthis,
When your flower was in place.
You seemed a gawky girl then, artless,
Without grace.

Atthis, you looked at what I was
And hated what you saw
And now, all in a flutter, chase
After Andromeda.

These three fragments show the speaker in various sorts of relationships with others – she is frustrated and flattered and then flatters in turn. 'Because' consists of a gnomic (general and proverbial) statement and probably belonged to a poem that related a specific instance of unrequited love. The speaker's advances have come to nothing, and she may have called for divine aid, as in 'Subtly bedizened Aphrodite'.

In 'By giving me creations of their own' the girls give the speaker *timē* – a word which means both honour and value. In Homer's *Iliad*, *timē* is talked about as if it were a physical object. Agamemnon, for example, takes *timē* away from Achilles when he appropriates the concubine Briseïs in Book 1 of the *Iliad*. As in the Homeric world the girls here publicly acknowledge Sappho's value by awarding her prizes. These gifts, however, are special because Sappho has inspired their creation, and her own value is literally coming home to her.

'And this next charming ditty I' is charming indeed. The singer cleverly suggests that her girls are as pretty as the song being performed in their honour. She is clearly addressing an audience, i.e. this is a public performance for people other than herself and her girls. The girls were probably present at the performance as well, as dancers who accompanied the song.

... because
The people I most strive to please
Do me the worst injuries ...

By giving me creations of their own
My girls have handed me renown.

And this next charming ditty I –
In honour of my girls –
Shall sing out prettily.

Sappho does not merely study the experience of love and loss in others but actively participates. Here the speaker in a song elides distinctions between herself and Abanthis by bidding her take up the lyre, and desire moves through them both. She takes sympathetic pleasure in Abanthis' arousal over Gongyla's flattering attire. As each character is both subject and object, this song perfectly exemplifies the 'circular, Sapphic law according to which beauty demands love and love, in turn, creates the beautiful' (Burnett 1983, p. 229).

In its triangular arrangement of singer, addressee and absent girl, the fragment operates as 'Off in Sardis' does. However, by gazing at an object (a flattering garment and the girl admiring the garment) Abanthis and the speaker experience a physical reaction comparable to the speaker's reactions in 'That fellow strikes me as god's double', another song with a triangular arrangement of characters. The manuscript falls apart just at the turn – we learn that Aphrodite has censured the speaker for an inappropriate prayer. That last legible word is a tantalizing '. . . I wish . . .' André Lardinois speculates that performance involved exchanges between Sappho or another soloist and a chorus and expressed a collective desire for the absent Gongyla (1996, p. 170).

'As you are dear to me, go claim a younger' is a mysterious fragment. On the assumption that the speaker is addressing a male, Stobaeus (fifth century CE) comments in a gloss that 'in marriage the age of the partners should be considered' (4.22.112). We cannot determine the gender of the speaker and addressee or the original context.

Abanthis, please pick up your lyre,
Praise Gongyla. Your need to sing
Flutters about you in the air –
You gorgeous thing.

Her garment (when you stole a glance)
Roused you, and I'm in ecstasy.
Likewise, the goddess Kypris once
Disciplined me

Blaming the way I prayed . . .

As you are dear to me, go claim a younger
Bed as your due.
I can't stand being the old one any longer,
Living with you.

In 2004 Michael Gronewald and Robert Daniel announced the identification of a papyrus in the University of Cologne as part of a roll containing poems of Sappho. This song was copied early in the third century BCE and later served as Egyptian mummy cartonnage. Its discovery provided the left-hand side of a poem whose right-hand side had been known since 1922 from an Oxyrhynchus papyrus, also of the third century BCE. The two texts together form a nearly complete poem.

The focus is on Sappho herself. She lists the symptoms of her ageing as she does those of desire in 'That fellow strikes me as god's double'. A singer probably performed this song while a chorus danced, and the poem becomes more poignant if we imagine Sappho complaining of age while her girls 'pranced nimbly' as fawns around her.

The Muses here are 'violet-bosomed' like the bride in 'And may the maidens all night long' and Dawn is 'rosy-forearmed' like the Graces in 'Untainted Graces'. In the last four lines Sappho cites the story of Dawn and Tithonous as an exemplum (myth used as evidence). The goddess Dawn takes the beautiful youth Tithonous as her husband and then spirits him away to the eastern edge of the known world from which she rises every morning. At her request Zeus grants Tithonous immortality but she forgets to ask for eternal youth as well, and he withers away with age. In some accounts he merely chatters and is too weak to move; in others he turns into a cricket.

The old and withered Tithonous recounts his sad decay in Alfred Lord Tennyson's dramatic monologue *Tithonus* (1860), 15–23; in this version, however, it is Dawn herself, rather than Zeus, who gives her lover eternal life:

> I asked thee, 'Give me immortality.'
> Then didst thou grant mine asking with a smile,
> Like wealthy men who care not how they give.
> But thy strong Hours indignant worked their wills,
> And beat me down and marred and wasted me,
> And though they could not end me, left me maimed
> To dwell in presence of immortal youth,
> Immortal age beside immortal youth,
> And all I was, in ashes.

Girls, chase the violet-bosomed Muses' bright
Gifts and the plangent lyre, lover of hymns:

Stiffness has seized on these once supple limbs,
And black braids with the passing years turned white.

Age weighs heavily on me, and the knees
Buckle that long ago, like fawns, pranced nimbly.

I groan much but to what end? Humans simply
Cannot be ageless like divinities.

They say that rosy-forearmed Dawn, when stung
With love, swept a sweet youth to the earth's rim –

Tithonous. Even there age withered him,
Bound still to a wife forever young.

Sappho's eldest brother Charaxus exported wine to Naucratis in Egypt, a Greek settlement and trading post established *c.* 615–610 BCE. There he became attached to a courtesan named Doricha. The historian Herodotus confuses Doricha with a later and more famous courtesan named Rhodope and mistakenly assigns the affair to the reign of Amasis II (570–526 BCE) (II.134f.). In 'Kypris, may Doricha discover' Sappho entreats Kyprian Aphrodite (or Aphrodite of Cyprus) to punish Doricha for having entangled a man, most likely her brother.

Sappho invokes the same goddess in 'Nereids, Kypris, please restore', along with the Nereids, the sea deities who had a cult centre on Lesbos. This fragment was part of a *propempticon* or bon voyage poem. We soon learn, however, that Charaxus' past behaviour has clearly been a source of embarrassment for Sappho and their family. Therefore she asks also that her wayward brother mend his ways and behave in accordance with the heroic code by helping his family and friends and harming his enemies. What begins as prayer for safe travel trails off with 'gloomy' misgivings concerning her brother's future. After an initial first-person singular ('My brother') Sappho uses the first-person plural to include other members of her family and/or friends and perhaps also a chorus which danced while the song was performed.

Ancient sources inform us that Sappho composed invective against her brother Charaxus but nothing harsher than this fragment has survived.

Kypris, may Doricha discover
You are the bitterest thing of all
And not keep boasting that a lover
Twice came to call.

Nereids, Kypris, please restore
My brother to this port, unkilled.
May all his heart most wishes for
Now be fulfilled.

Excuse the misdeeds in his past,
Make him his friends' boon and foes' bane,
And may we never find the least
Cause to complain.

May he choose to give his sister
Her share of honour but my gloomy
Misgivings . . .

Ancient biographies attest that Sappho had a daughter named Kleïs. She may well have, but we should admit that our evidence – 'I have a daughter that reminds me of' – is not conclusive: *pais* (which I have translated as 'daughter') can mean either 'child' or 'slave', and the speaker of the poem may not have been Sappho. Here, as in 'But I love extravagance' the speaker possesses something of even greater value than the luxuries she esteems. This fragment is one of several in which Sappho sets up an alternative marketplace in which desire, beauty and the people who inspire or possess them are more valuable than luxury items and other commodities.

'I do not have an' may belong to Sappho's exile to Sicily or to Pittacus' ten-year rule in Mytilene (595–585 BCE), during which he passed laws prohibiting some luxuries. The speaker does not address Kleïs as if she were a slave, and the fragment makes the most sense if we imagine her as a young girl whining for the accessories to which she had been accustomed. This fragment is preserved on a third-century-BCE papyrus (one of the oldest manuscripts) along with 'You see, my mother'.

I have a daughter who reminds me of
A marigold in bloom.
Kleïs is her name,
And I adore her.
I would refuse all Lydia's glitter for her
And all other love.

I do not have an
Ornately woven
Bandeau to hand you,
Kleïs. From
Where would it come?

The *Suda* biography informs us that Sappho's mother's name was Kleïs. Since daughters were to be named after grandmothers as sons were after grandfathers, the biographer may have first concluded the name of Sappho's *pais* was Kleïs and then, for just this reason, assumed her grandmother's was Kleïs too. Still, he may have had access to more information than we do. For feminine apparel Sardis was the Paris of the ancient Aegean. This fragment runs through a complete cycle of fashion: from outmoded ornate headbands to simple floral garlands and back again.

... You see, my mother,

Back when she was young,
Thought it was fancy for a girl to wear
A purple fillet, a headband –

Yes, this was quite the thing.
Now, though, we have seen a girl with hair
More orange than a firebrand

Sport all the flowers of spring
Woven together, garlands upon garlands –
And only lately, fresh from Sardis,

A spangled headband ...

Athenaeus explains that 'the towels [mentioned in this poem] are a decorative head-covering, as Hecataeus, or whoever wrote the travel-account entitled *The Asia*, evinces: "The women wear towels on their heads"' (*Scholars at Dinner* 9.410e). Ancient Greek clothing consisted mostly of swaths of cloth of various lengths and widths which could serve a variety of functions. As we have seen accessories were important to Sappho's group as status symbols.

I was delighted to learn that 'A handkerchief' has acquired a cult status in some literary critical circles – it is tantalizing and elliptical. *Aimitybion*, the word Sappho uses for 'handkerchief', refers to a piece of cloth smaller than our towels and of some thinner material, such as linen. This rare word appears again in Aristophanes' comedy *Wealth*, 729 (388 BCE): 'he took out a clean handkerchief and wiped his eyes'. In this fragment the cloth is dual-purpose, capable of serving both as a handkerchief and a bandana. What, however, is the handkerchief dripping? Why is it dripping at all? Parallels for the word 'dripping' (*stalasson*, related to 'stalagmite') suggest that the liquid is probably blood, sweat or tears.

Mnasis sent you from Phocaia
Purple kerchiefs you can tie
Around your brow to serve
As headscarves, too –
Rich gifts which you,
With your fine cheeks, deserve.

A handkerchief
Dripping with . . .

TROY

Mythic narratives are rare in Sappho, with the exception of events from the Trojan saga. I have gathered into this section those fragments which either narrate events pertaining to this war or cite stories from it as exempla (myths used as evidence). Sappho here uses a distinctly Homeric ambience, that is – an objective viewpoint and a dactylic metre suggestive of the metre of Homer's *Iliad* and *Odyssey*. The fragment relates the almost telepathic spread of *kleos* (renown) through the Trojan community. *Kleos* is the reputation a Homeric character 'enjoys among his or her contemporaries, or "what is said" of that individual and his or her deeds . . .' (Douglas Olson, *Blood and Iron: Stories and Storytelling in Homer's Odyssey* (1995), p. 3).

It is striking that Sappho chooses a conventionally 'feminine' theme, a wedding scene which has no parallel in Homer. Though she elevates the wedding to epic magnitude, she does not moralize about the fates of Hector (whom Achilles kills), Andromache (who is given as booty to Achilles' son, Neoptolemos) and their child Astyanax (who is flung from the walls of Troy). As Wilson points out: 'there is no good and evil in [this song], merely a superlative state that could be defined as excellence' (1996, p. 154).

Idaos is the principal herald for the Trojans in the *Iliad*. Though the setting is mythic, many of the details come from Sappho's time: *krotala* (rattles or castanets) do not appear in Homer, and myrrh, cassia and frankincense do not appear in Greek literature before her. I have translated the Greek *aulos* as 'double-oboe' to give an impression of the instrument's appearance and sound. With the merger of the Trojans and guests from Mysian Thebes, we have a mingling of sounds and scents. The singers are of all ages, all classes and both genders. The final *makarismos* (or blessing in which the couple are compared to gods) dissolves a further division between mortals and immortals.

A soloist probably performed this song while playing a lyre. We are told that it was an epithalamium, and it may well have been performed at a wedding banquet.

Idaos, then, the panting emissary,
Reported:
          'Out of Asia deathless glory:
From holy Thebe and the stream-fed port
Of Plakia, Hector and his men escort
The bright-eyed, delicate Andromache
On shipboard over the infertile sea –
With sweet red garments, bracelets made of gold,
Beautiful baubles, ivory and untold
Chalices chased in silver.' So he spoke.

Dear Priam rose at once, and the news broke,
Spreading to friends throughout the city's wide
Expanse. And soon the sons of Ilos tied
Pack mules to smooth-wheeled carts, and whole
          parades
Clambered aboard the transports – wives and maids
With slim-tapering ankles. Some way off,
The daughters of King Priam stood aloof,
And youthful stewards harnessed teams of horses
To chariots . . .

. . . And sweetly then the double-oboe's cadence
Mingled with rhythmic rattles as the maidens
Sang sacred songs. A fine sound strode the air.
Cups on the roadside, vessels everywhere,
Cassia and frankincense were mixed with myrrh.
Old women (venerable as they were)
Warbled and trilled. The men all in a choir
Summoned first that lover of the lyre,
The long-range archer, Paeon, then extolled
Andromache and Hector, godlike to behold.

The first stanza contains a priamel, a literary focusing device in which alternatives serve as foils for the true subject of the poem, revealed as the climax. Pindar's *First Olympian Ode* begins with an elaborate priamel highlighting the Olympic games:

> Water is best, and gold, like a fire blazing at night,
> Outshines all lordly wealth. But, O my heart,
> If you wish to extol great competitions,
> Look no further for any star warmer than the sun
> Shining by day through the empty sky
> Or for a contest greater than the Olympics.
>
> (1–8)

In Sappho's fragment military divisions serve as foils leading up to the climactic declaration: the 'most beautiful' thing is 'whatever a person most lusts after'.

On the assumption that this fragment is a straightforward love poem for Anaktoria, translators have often rendered the climactic line of the first stanza: 'whomever one loves'. There are a number of problems with this: first, the verb is *eratai*, which is related to Eros and expresses a strong physical desire. Eros is almost always an irrational, destructive force, and the meaning of the verb is much closer to 'lust after' than 'feel love for'. Second, this lust is directed at an indefinite and neuter object of desire, not 'whomever' but 'whatever'. More than simply a love song, this poem is a quasi-philosophical treatise on the abstract notion of desire.

Further confusion has resulted from reading Helen as love object instead of active subject. She decides of her own free will to give up her husband and family for a person that she desires. Her object of desire, Paris, is not named in what we have of the poem, and this omission better serves the initial philosophical proposition. Dubois sees this poem as 'one of the few texts which break the silence of women in antiquity, an instant in which women become more than the objects of man's desire' (1996, p. 79). The audience is left to decide whether Helen's voluntary abandonment of her family is reprehensible or justifiable.

Some call ships, infantry or horsemen
The greatest beauty earth can offer;
I say it is whatever a person
Most lusts after.

Showing you all will be no trouble:
Helen surpassed all humankind
In looks but left the world's most noble
Husband behind,

Coasting off to Troy where she
Thought nothing of her loving parents
And only child but, led astray . . .

. . . and I think of Anaktoria
Far away, . . .

And I would rather watch her body
Sway, her glistening face flash dalliance
Than Lydian war cars at the ready
And armed battalions.

As Sappho revises the traditional account of Helen's arrival at Troy, so here she further alters the backstory: everyone must have heard, or so the speaker claims, that Leda simply found the egg from which her children (including Helen) were born. In the standard version Leda is impregnated both by Zeus (in the form of a swan) and her husband Tyndareus. She gives birth to two eggs: one containing Helen and Polydeuces (Zeus' children) and another with Clytemnestra and Castor (Tyndareus' children).

'Reveal your graceful figure here' breaks down into the traditional tripartite structure of a kletic hymn (see Introduction, p. xxvi). The Atreidae, or sons of Atreus, are: Agamemnon, king of Mycenae and leader of the expedition to Troy, and his brother Menelaus, king of Sparta and husband of Helen. Here, after having sacked Troy on the north-western coast of Asia Minor (modern Turkey), the brothers have stopped on Lesbos and are attempting to depart for their homeward journey.

In *Odyssey* 3.130–46 Nestor tells a story of a quarrel between Agamemnon and Menelaus. While Agamemnon decides to stay with half of the army at Troy to make sacrifice to the goddess Athena, Menelaus departs immediately with the others and then stops at Lesbos to contemplate the rest of the voyage and pray to Zeus. In Sappho's account the brothers are travelling together, and the Athenian playwright Aeschylus (525/4–456/5 BCE) follows this version (*Agamemnon* 617–79). Rather than praying to Zeus alone, the brothers here pray to Zeus, Hera and Dionysos ('Thyone's charming son'). Alcaeus sings of the foundation of a shrine on Lesbos in honour of these three divinities:

> 'the Lesbians founded the great conspicuous precinct here to be kept in common. They put altars of the blessed immortals in it, and they named Zeus God of Suppliants and you, the glorious goddess of Aeolia, Mother of All, and third Kemelios, Dionysos, raw-flesh-eater . . .'
>
> (129.1–9 Voigt)

In our fragment the text breaks off before we learn the content of Sappho's prayer. She may have prayed for fair winds during a friend's voyage.

Yes, you have all heard
That Leda, long ago, one day
Noticed an egg, hyacinth-coloured,
Hidden away.

Reveal your graceful figure here,
Close to me, Hera. I make entreaty
Just as the kings once made their prayer,
The famous Atreidai –

Winning victories by the score
At Troy first, then at sea, they sailed
The channel to this very shore,
Tried leaving but failed

Until they prayed to you, the Saviour
Zeus and Thyone's charming son.
Like long ago, then, grant this favour,
As you have done . . .

MAIDENS AND MARRIAGES

Sappho frequently mingles eroticism and innocence, and 'Once as a too, too lissome' could serve as a motto for this series of fragments. Throughout Western literature maidens are identified with flowers, and the *Homeric Hymn to Demeter*, roughly contemporary with the works of Sappho, makes this identification explicit: 'the narcissus which Earth bore as a lure for the flower-faced girl' (10). Persephone's rape by Hades (or Dis), god of the underworld, serves as the prototype of all such ravishment. Maidens who died before their wedding day are often portrayed in art and literature as brides of Death. John Milton (1608–74) recounts the rape of Persephone (or Proserpina):

> Not that fair field
> Of Enna, where Proserpin gath'ring flow'rs
> Herself a fairer flower by gloomy Dis
> Was gather'd ...
> *(Paradise Lost, 4.268–71)*

William Shakespeare (1564–1616) makes Death's defloration of the maiden even more explicit. Old Capulet, believing that his daughter Juliet is dead, states:

> There she lies,
> Flower as she was, deflowered by him.
> Death is my son-in-law, Death is my heir;
> My daughter he hath wedded ...
> *(Romeo and Juliet, Act 4, Scene 5)*

In Greek literature the culling of flowers indicates that a girl is ready for marriage. The maiden, however, is most tempting at this time, and her plucking of a bloom often leads to her own deflowering. She is both defenceless and seductive.

Artemis, along with Athena and Hestia, remains a virgin goddess, a deity over whom Aphrodite has no sway. Sappho gives a Homeric air to 'Artemis made the pledge no god can break' by using epic diction and rhythms. We find a nearly identical scene, involving Zeus and Hestia, Goddess of the Hearth, in the *Homeric Hymn to Aphrodite* (21–8):

The works of Aphrodite do not delight the pure virgin Hestia ... both Poseidon and Apollo courted her but she was wholly unwilling, she staunchly refused; laying her hand on the head of Father Zeus ... she swore an oath that she would remain a virgin eternally, and indeed it has come to pass.

Once as a too, too lissome
Maiden was plucking a blossom . . .

Artemis made the pledge no god can break:
'Upon my head and all that I hold dear,
I shall remain a maid, a mountaineer
Hunting on summits – grant this for my sake.'

The Father of the Blessèd gave the nod – yes;
And all the gods pronounced her Frontier Goddess
And Slayer of Stags, and Eros never crosses
Her path . . .

These two similes, 'A ripe red apple grows, the highest of them all' and 'A hillside hyacinth shepherds treaded flat', are both composed in a metre called dactylic hexameter, used in hymns, epithalamia and epic. The Roman poet Catullus adapts them in poem 62, in which choirs of boys and maidens sing in response to each other and which may well be an adaptation of a longer poem by Sappho which included these two similes (see 'Hesperus, you are'). Like flowers, apples in particular and fruit in general are associated with maidens. In Aeschylus' tragedy *The Suppliants* (produced *c.* 463 BCE) Danaos expounds upon the association of fruit and maidenhood in a warning to his daughters:

> . . . I urge you not to slip and fall, my dears.
> Remember how flagrantly you have attained
> The buxom age that turns the heads of men.
> A ripe fruit is not easy to protect.
> Winged scavengers and every beast with feet
> To slink on – yes, I mean men also – ache
> To tear it from the branch. How could they not,
> When Aphrodite injects such succulence
> That pulp comes plumping out beneath the rind?
> Tempting, a maiden's rondure is, the target
> Of every eye, and fingers cannot help
> But to reach out and pluck.
>
> (996–1005)

In 'Maidenhead, maidenhead, where have you gone?' a former maiden has been separated from a part of herself, and this part, personified as Maidenhood itself, drives the separation home with a mocking, almost ghoulish response. Sappho also uses personification in 'God-crafted product of the tortoise shell'. The Greek rhetorician Demetrius (first century CE) singles this fragment out for praise, commenting on Sappho's use of repetition 'where a bride speaks to her virginity, and it answers her using the same device' (*On Style* 140).

(I)

A ripe red apple grows, the highest of them all,
Over the treetop, way up on a tapering spray,
But apple-gatherers never see it – no,
Rather, they *do* see it is far away,
Beyond their reach, impossible.
This matter stands just so.

(II)

A hillside hyacinth shepherds treaded flat,
A red bloom in the dust – it is like that.

'Maidenhead, maidenhead, where have you gone?'

'I shall never, ever join you again.'

I combined two related fragments to make 'Hesperus, you are'.
Hesperus is a personification of the planet Venus, known as the
Evening Star when it appears at dusk. Catullus adapts these lines,
along with 'A ripe red apple grows, the highest of them all', in poem
62. A chorus of maidens inverts the imagery of Sappho's song:

> Hesperus, what more cruel fire than yours moves in the sky?
> You tear a daughter from her mother's arms,
> From her mother's arms tear a clinging daughter,
> And give a chaste maid to an ardent youth.
> What worse acts do enemies perform when a city falls?
> *Hymn, O Hymenaeus, Hymn, approach, Hymenaeus.*   (20–25)

A chorus of boys responds:

> Hesperus, what more delightful fire than yours shines in the sky?
> With your flame you validate the contracted engagements
> Which husbands and parents have pledged beforehand
> But do not consummate until your flame has appeared.
> What do the gods grant that is more desirable than this blessed hour?
> *Hymn, O Hymenaeus, Hymn, approach, Hymenaeus.*   (26–31)

The nightingale becomes a symbol of poetry and lamentation in
Western literature. According to tradition, King Tereus of Thrace,
while escorting his wife Procne's sister, Philomela, back to his palace,
rapes the girl and cuts out her tongue to prevent her from accusing
him. Philomela weaves a tapestry to show her sister the crime and, in
revenge, Procne kills her son Itylus and feeds him to Tereus. Tereus
chases them until the gods transform them all into birds: Tereus
into a hawk; Philomela, a swallow; and Procne, a nightingale forever
grieving for her son. In later sources Philomela is the nightingale, and
her sister the swallow.

Homer, himself described as the Nightingale of Chios, alludes to
the tale of Philomela (*Odyssey* 19.512–24), and the Greek tragedian
Sophocles calls the nightingale the 'messenger of Zeus' because it
signals the coming of spring (*Electra* 149). Algernon Charles Swin-
burne portrays a nightingale as Philomela in a chorus from his tragedy
Atalanta in Calydon (1865):

> And the brown bright nightingale amorous
> Is half assuaged for Itylus,
> For the Thracian ships and the foreign faces,
> The tongueless vigil, and all the pain.

Hesperus, you are
The most fetching star.
What Dawn flings afield
You bring back together –
Sheep to the fold, goats to the pen,
And the child to his mother again.

Nightingale,
All you sing
Is desire;
You are the crier
Of coming spring.

Here a speaker representing a group en route to a wedding asks an older woman to impart her wisdom. An anticipatory excitement suffuses those epithalamia set before the ceremony itself. One gets the feeling that we should 'pack the maids off quickly' only so that there will be more weddings in the near future, and the speaker talks of weddings as if they were an end in themselves. Indeed, for a Greek female, all of her life leads either towards this one event or away from it. Burnett cites this fragment as evidence for the importance of female role-models in Sappho's group and argues that songs such as this taught the girls of the community 'just what to do' (1983, p. 218). The shift in focus to deities at the end of the translated text is curious. All that we can make out from the subsequent text is the elliptical phrase: '[no?] road to great Olympus for mortals'. Choral performance is standard for epithalamia and the speaker exhorting the woman to 'Talk to us for a spell' is almost certainly a chorus.

Because once on a time you were
Young, sing of what is taking place,
Talk to us for a spell, confer
Your special grace.

For we march to a wedding – yes,
You know it well. So pack the maids off
Quickly, and may the gods possess . . .

A chorus probably sang 'Groomsmen, kings with bastions' during the procession from the father of the bride's house to the groom's house. The groomsmen are compared to kings with hilltop fortresses and exhorted to keep the bride impregnable until she arrives safely at her new home.

'It would take seven fathoms to span' is the first in a series of bawdy wedding songs which turn on phallic double entendre. On what happened when the bride and groom retired to the wedding chamber, see Introduction, pp. xxix–xxx.

Groomsmen, kings with bastions
In strong positions,
Keep this bride
Well fortified.

It would take seven fathoms to span
The feet of the doorkeeper (the best man);
His sandals are five cows' worth of leather
And ten shoemakers stitched them together.

In 'What do you resemble, dear husband-to-be?' the answer (a sapling) suggests both the youth of the groom and the 'family tree' that will grow from him. Genital joking is not far beneath the surface of this fragment as well.

Sappho presents us with a paradox at the end of 'Carpenters, raise the rafter-beam' – the groom is bigger than a big man. The audience is left to riddle out the hyberbole, and the answer is inevitably that he has an erection which extends so far above his head that the roof must be raised. Compare the anonymous phallic song: 'Get up and give the god some room to grow, for the god – upright, in full throb – longs to pass through our midst' (Denys Page, *Poetae Melici Graeci* (1962), 851a). Refrains such as 'For Hymen's wedding hymn' are common in epithalamia and appear in a number of the wedding poems of Theocritus and Catullus (see 'May you bed down' and 'Hesperus, you are').

'What do you resemble, dear husband-to-be?'

'You resemble a supple seedling, a green tree.'

> Carpenters, raise the rafter-beam
> (For Hymen's wedding hymn)
> A little higher to make room
> (For Hymen's wedding hymn)
> Because here comes the groom –
> An Ares more imposing than
> A giant, a terribly big man.

For 'Blest bridegroom, this day of matrimony' I have done my best to preserve the ceremonial effects of rhythm, repetition and alliteration. After the ellipsis the rapid accumulation of the bride's attractions in the Greek equivalent of a run-on sentence achieves an effect similar to the list of symptoms in 'That fellow strikes me as god's double'. Eros, however, ceases to be destructive in a matrimonial context but is 'enlisted in the service of the social institutions that make for continuity and stability' (Segal 1996, p. 71). Here we find an intimate and even eroticizing description of the bride in a public wedding performance. The ending of this fragment may be a *makarismos*. In the last line we learn that Aphrodite has graced the bride with immortal beauty, just as goddesses enhance the appearance of certain heroes in Homer's *Iliad* and *Odyssey*.

'The ambrosial mixture' presents an immortal wedding scene, perhaps the marriage of Peleus and Thetis (the parents of the hero Achilles). This fragment is exceptional in that no females are mentioned and we are left with an impression of male solidarity. The customary cup-bearers for the gods are Hebe (the daughter of Zeus and Hera) and Ganymede (a Trojan prince carried off to Olympus by Zeus). Here, as in a song by Sappho's contemporary Alcaeus, Hermes is serving as cup-bearer. There is a certain irony in the drink offerings which the wedding guests pour on to the ground – since at least some of them are gods, they are pouring offerings to themselves.

Blest bridegroom, this day of matrimony,
Just as you wished it, has come true:
The bride is whom you wished for . . .

                               'You
Move gracefully; your eyes are honey;
Charm was showered on your radiant face –
Yes, Aphrodite granted you outstanding praise.'

The ambrosial mixture
Ready in the mixing bowl,
Hermes went round with a pitcher
And served the gods. When all
Had tipped their goblets and poured offerings,
They prayed that the groom suffer only the good
      things.

In 'Because there is no other bride than she' the speaker acts as
salesperson for a bride who is still a *pais* (child). The proper age for
marriage is a recurring theme in Greek literature. The poet Hesiod
(*c.* 700 BCE) gives this advice in *Works and Days*: 'Make sure your
bride has been grown up for four years, and marry her in the fifth.
And be sure to marry a virgin, so that you can school her in useful
habits' (698–9).

Imagery of the moon surrounded by star clusters has a long history in
Western literature, and this note will only cover the beginning of it.
Homer compares the Trojan watchfires around Hector to stars around
a moon: 'The stars around the shining moon are pre-eminently bright'
(*Iliad* 8.555). Eustathius of Thessalonica (1110–98 CE) in his commen-
tary on the *Iliad* notes that 'in the expression "around the shining
moon" one should not understand the light of the full moon; for then
the stars are dim because they are outshone'. The image of a full moon
eclipsing surrounding stars is not attested before Sappho. Bacchylides
(*c.* 507 – *c.* 450 BCE) adapts it for an ode in honour of a victor in the
pentathlon (consisting of discus, javelin, long jump, foot race and
wrestling events): 'He shined among his fellow pentathletes / as the
beautiful moon on a mid-month night / outshines the light of stars'
(9.27–8). If this fragment of Sappho were, in fact, part of an epitha-
lamium, a solo singer or chorus of maidens would here be praising
the bride in much the same way.

'And may the maidens all night long' was probably sung outside the
wedding chamber. A chorus of bridesmaids is exhorting one of the
groomsmen to invite his friends to the groom's house to keep watch
with them before the door. The bride has a violet bosom like the
Muses in 'Girls, chase the violet-bosomed Muses' bright'. 'The bird
that intones / Piercing moans' is the nightingale (see 'Nightingale') but
also evokes the bride on the wedding night.

Because there is no other girl than she,
Bridegroom – a child still, of such quality.

Star clusters near the fair moon dim
Their shapely shimmering whenever
She rises, lucent to the brim
And flowing over.

And may the maidens all night long
Celebrate your shared love in song
And the bride's bosom,
A violet-blossom.

Get up, now! Rouse that gang of fellows –
Your boys – and we shall sleep as well as
The bird that intones
Piercing moans.

THE WISDOM OF SAPPHO

Aristotle defines a *gnomē* as 'a statement not about particular things, such as what sort of man Iphicrates is, but about generalities, and not about all things, such as that straight is the opposite of crooked, but about kinds of actions and whether they should be taken or avoided' (*Rhetoric* 1394a21–6). In short, it offers general advice much like a proverb. Two of the most famous *gnomai* were written in the entry to the Temple of Apollo at Delphi: 'Nothing in excess' and 'Know thyself.' Whereas each phrase or line on its own might sound banal, what is important in gnomic poetry is the combination. The poet displays his or her art in the joining of them.

In addition to implying that beauty is more than skin deep, 'The gorgeous man presents a gorgeous view' suggests a sublimation of mere visual appeal, inasmuch as goodness has its beauty as well. This fragment is to be compared with 'whatever a person / Most lusts after' in 'Some call ships, infantry or horsemen'. An anonymous ancient commentator preserves 'Wealth without real worthiness' in his explication of a *gnomē* in Pindar's *Second Olympian Ode*: 'Wealth decorated with virtues brings all kinds of opportunities' (96–7).

In *Figures of Speech* the Greek grammarian Tryphon (late first century BCE) cites 'Neither the honey nor the bee' as an example of a proverb, and the anthologist Diogenian (early second century CE) explains in his work on *Proverbs* that it 'is used of those who are unwilling to take the good along with the bad'. The original is *mēte moi meli mēte melissa*. I was unable to preserve its striking alliteration.

The gorgeous man presents a gorgeous view;
The good man will in time be gorgeous, too.

Wealth without real worthiness
Is no good for the neighbourhood;
But their proper mixture is
The summit of beatitude.

Neither the honey nor the bee
For me . . .

These three fragments consist of dilemmas and alternatives. 'I want to tell you something but good taste' was composed in the Alcaic stanza, named after Sappho's contemporary who frequently employed it. Aristotle informs us that it is poetic 'correspondence', the first line and a half composed by Alcaeus and the rest by Sappho. Sappho uses the Alcaic stanza because it is the preferred metre of her correspondent and the one in which the original comment was written. Thus, Alcaeus' poem prompted a response much as Christopher Marlowe's 'The Passionate Shepherd to His Love' did Sir Walter Raleigh's 'The Nymph's Reply to the Shepherd'. The Greek *aidōs*, which I have translated as 'good taste', 'bears a certain surface resemblance to what we call "respect", but is distinguished from it by the fact that its implications are essentially negative, so that it normally restrains action rather than requiring it' (Douglas Olson, *Blood and Iron: Stories and Storytelling in Homer's Odyssey* (1995), p. 17). Aristotle cites this fragment in support of his claim that 'men are ashamed to speak of, do and intend shameful things' (*Rhetoric* 1367a).

The Greek grammarian Apollonius Dyscolus (fl. second century CE) cites 'Either I have slipped out of your head' in a treatise on *Pronouns* because it contains a dialectical variant of the first-person singular. The fragment captures the fatalistic mindset of the lover. Certain that she has been scorned, the lover only wonders why.

The Stoic philosopher Chrysippus of Soli (*c.* 280–207 BCE) preserves 'I don't know what the right course is' in a treatise *On Negatives*.

'I want to tell you something but good taste
Restrains me.'
                    'If you wanted to express
Some noble or gorgeous thought – that is, unless
Your tongue were keen to utter in hot haste
Some shameful slur, "good taste" would not have
     dressed
Your face in red, no, you would have professed
Whatever you would say upfront and straightaway.'

Either I have slipped out of your head
Or you adore some fellow more, instead.

I don't know what the right course is;
Twofold are my purposes.

'I declare' appears near the end of a *Discourse* wrongly ascribed to the Greek orator, writer and historian Dio Chrysostum (*c.* 40 – *c.* 120 CE). Upset that a statue of him has been taken down, the speaker (who has yet to be identified with any certainty) learnedly lectures the Corinthians on immortality through art. In Sappho's case at least, the claim has turned out to be true.

I declare
That later on,
Even in an age unlike our own,
Someone will remember who we are.

APPENDIX:
TWO NEW POEMS

In 2013 an as yet unnamed private collector in London showed a scrap of papyrus from mummy wrapping to Dr Dirk Obbink, a papyrologist at Oxford University. Based on dialect, meter and internal references, Obbink identified the poems as 'indubitably . . . by Sappho in her first book' (Obbink 2014). The provenance of the papyrus is unknown but, however it was acquired, we should be grateful it was made public. The scrap contains two poems: the first, here, which is missing its opening lines, and a second which gives us only an opening five lines before the text breaks down and becomes indecipherable. In what we have of the first poem, a speaker, let's say Sappho, is talking to someone, perhaps her mother Kleïs, about Sappho's brother Charaxus (See 'Nereids, Kypris, please restore'). He is a wine-merchant who sails frequently for work, has been gone a long time and, according to tradition, is involved with a lover Doricha abroad (See 'Kypris, may Doricha discover'). Also mentioned is a younger brother Larichus. The poem fits in well with others of Sappho's family-drama poems. The context evokes Homer's *Odyssey*, with the absent sea-faring Charaxus representing Odysseus, and the young Larichus, Odysseus' son Telemachus.

For this and the next translation, I used the text of Dirk Obbink, 'Two New Poems From Sappho', *Zeitschrift für Papyrologie und Epigraphik* (*ZPE*) 189 (2014).

... You're always babbling

Charaxus, he's come home again!
His ship's hold full! But if he will
is known to Zeus and gods alone.
Don't think of him at all,

but make me do it, send me forth
to beg and beg Queen Hera *Please*
let him come safely to his berth,
his vessel in one piece,

and find us well. For all things else
we need to trust in deities.
All in a moment mighty squalls
give way to peaceful days.

Those whom Olympian Zeus has given
a good-luck god and made secure
from toil, they have a lavish living
and joy beyond compare,

and then there's us. If Larichus
one day should hold his head up high
and be a man, our countless woes
would lift and leave us free.

These lines, the beginning of a new poem, appear beneath 'You're always babbling' on the recently published scrap of papyrus. Sappho is here addressing/conversing with Kyprian Aphrodite, as she does in other poems of an erotic nature. (See 'Leave Crete and sweep to this blest temple' and 'Subtly bedizened Aphrodite'.) The text breaks down at the end of the sixth line, and there is no clear grammar for the final sentence. I have translated those floating words with ellipses. With its generalizing, almost philosophical opening sentence, this fragment is comparable to 'Some call ships, infantry or horsemen'. The verb *dēïow*, which I have translated as 'stab', appears frequently in Homeric battle scenes, and it is likely that Sappho is again speaking of the concerns of her personal life in terms of the epic tradition. As the papyrus turns to tatters, the last four legible words are increasingly intense.

How could a person fail to ache,
Queen Kypris, always for the one
she loves and, more than anything,
wishes to welcome back again?

Please keep your eagerness in check,
since you have called me here, in vain,
to stab. . .desire. . .release. . .offspring. . .

Index of First Lines

LP   Edgar Lobel and Denys Page (eds.), *Poetarum Lesbiorum Fragmenta* (1955).
V   Eva-Maria Voigt (ed.), *Sappho et Alcaeus: Fragmenta* (1971).
W   Martin West, 'A New Sappho Poem', *Times Literary Supplement*, no. 5334 (24 June 2005), p. 8.
O   Dirk Obbink, 'Two New Poems from Sappho', *Zeitschrift für Papyrologie and Epigraphik* (ZPE) 189 (2014).

General Index